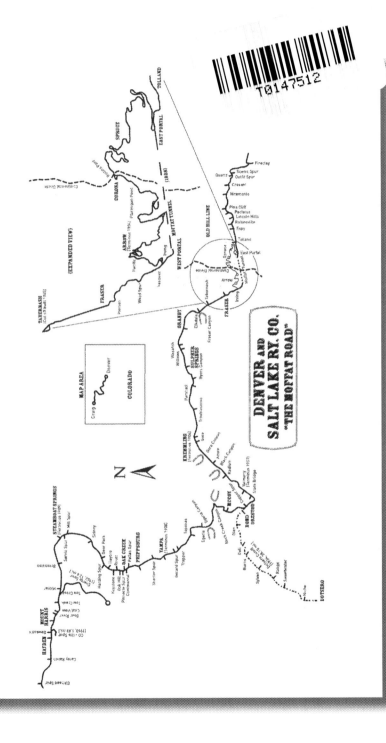

**Also by John A. Sells**

*Stagecoaches across the American West 1850–1920*

# THE MOFFAT LINE

## David Moffat's Railroad
## over and under the Continental Divide

### JOHN A. SELLS

iUniverse, Inc.
Bloomington

# The Moffat Line
## David Moffat's Railroad
## over and under the Continental Divide

*iUniverse books may be ordered through booksellers or by contacting:*

*iUniverse*
*1663 Liberty Drive*
*Bloomington, IN 47403*
*www.iuniverse.com*
*1-800-Authors (1-800-288-4677)*

*ISBN: 978-1-4620-2654-8 (sc)*
*ISBN: 978-1-4620-2655-5 (e)*
*ISBN: 978-1-4620-2656-2 (dj)*

*Printed in the United States of America*

*iUniverse rev. date: 9/1/2011*

# ACKNOWLEDGMENTS

Colorado Railroad Museum

Rollins Pass Restoration Association

The author is appreciative of the assistance of The New York Historical Society in New York City and the St. Joseph (Missouri) Museum and Library, and also of Kathy Camp, a Woolworth historian.

Manuscript material courtesy of Colorado Railroad Museum

# CONTENTS

*John A. Sells*

# PREFACE

Railroads contributed substantially to the development of Colorado during the last quarter of the nineteenth century and continue to do so. The unique geographic character of the state with its prairies and the Rocky Mountains required different methods of engineering and operating skills. The regions held all manner of minerals, oil, coal, and lumber, along with farming and ranching opportunities. The distances were manageable—if only travel could have been more efficient. David Moffat had a part in expanding railroads across western Colorado before he built one to run over the Continental Divide. There is a rich history of railroad exploits around the world operating in extreme situations, but there has never been the challenge of operating in an alpine environment with an around-the-clock itinerary. For those of us today, it was an impossible dream that led to the 1927 completion and 1928 opening of the six-mile (6.1) Moffat Tunnel—now a transcontinental link operated by Moffat's former adversary, the Union Pacific. This is a story that acknowledges David Halliday Moffat and the endless obstacles he faced. The story is also about the men who drove the trains and built and operated the railroad under incredible weather and equipment challenges—day and night. Without their courage and determination, this story could not have been written. The reader may find that the book jumps about a bit. It is intended to reflect the daily array of events. And it would be remiss to neglect recognition of Edward Taylor Bollinger and his encompassing *Rails That Climb*, first published in 1950.

# CHAPTER 1:
## MOFFAT BACKGROUND

This is a story about a man with a vision of a railroad going through a tunnel under the Continental Divide, but first David Moffat and his few loyal investors had to cross over the spine of the American continent. The Moffat family (spelled in a variety of ways) has two theories of origin. The simplest is directly to and from Scotland. The more detailed history finds the name progressing north from Italy, through France into Normandy, and then following William the Conqueror across the channel into England. From there, the thread leads to Scotland and, for some, over to Ireland. Today the representation is international.

The first Moffat to settle in the New World—Samuel and his wife Anne Gregg—sometime in the 1720s, located a spot on the upper Hudson River near present-day Newburgh, New York. Samuel and Anne had twelve children and all lived to at least adulthood, which was unusual for the time. Moreover, the Moffat progeny reportedly supported the Revolution during a divisive period and thereafter played a progressive part in business and local politics.

The early genealogy is set down in limited form in the McLaughlin book and in manuscript detail.[1] It is more than need be repeated here. Basically, the Moffat family—as it rapidly grew—was from all accounts a close-knit and productive group for over two hundred years, and there still remains a scattered linkage about the world. The centers of the American roots are Blooming Grove and Washingtonville, New York. The Washingtonville name was in deference to George Washington. The two towns and a museum and library exist today as one within the other. To the east is Newburgh, with State Road 208 serving as the artery, as it did in the early days as a rural road.

**Patriarchs**

David Halliday Moffat Sr., one of the twelve children born to Samuel and Anne Gregg, lived from March 1780 until October 1863. Some of the historical background suggests that he could barely support his large family of eight children. Besides farming, he owned a feed mill, which was twice destroyed by fire. Later, he reportedly was into premium butter production with another Moffat, and they marketed to New York City. As an aside, the oldest operating winery in the country, according to Moffat Library manuscripts, can be traced back to 1839 and John Jacques, a Moffat relation.

David H. Moffat Jr., one of eight children, was born July 23, 1839, and his childhood was spent among a growing Moffat family in Washingtonville. At the early age of eleven, he may have left home for New York City to work as a messenger for the New York Exchange Bank (now Irving Exchange bank). By age sixteen, he reportedly was an assistant to the bank teller. Although the real extent of his duties is not clear, it was not that uncommon for young people at the time to bear some significant responsibilities.

Samuel Moffat, the eldest child of David Moffat Jr., probably recalling the desperate times of his parents and his seven siblings, experienced the first call of the Western Frontier and moved to Des Moines, Iowa, in 1851 to take a bank cashier position. The community was founded in 1845 in a rich agricultural region. Samuel was soon writing letters encouraging any Moffat to pick up and relocate some 1,200 miles west to join him. Most seem to have passed on the invitation. However, his parents—along with his younger brother David Moffat Jr.—made the decision to go West, traveling in the comfort of the New York and Erie Railroad.

With Samuel's referral and David's New York Exchange Bank

experience, the transition probably went well enough. Employees with money management skills on the frontier were in short supply. While at the New York Exchange Bank, David Moffat Jr. had become a close friend of Benjamin F. Allen. Aside from Samuel, it may have been the influence of Allen that sealed Moffat's decision to go along with his family to Des Moines. While there, he worked at the A. J. Stevens Bank.

## On His Own

Benjamin Allen had bigger plans, however, and he soon moved 135 miles west to Omaha where he planned to establish a "financial center." Moffat soon followed Allen to Omaha and a job as cashier for the Bank of Nebraska. However, even with the tight family bonding, the raw frontier of Omaha was a world away from Des Moines and David Jr. left alone. Unknown to Moffat, he was at the right spot at the right time. In the later years, family members reportedly may have joined Moffat in Denver.

During his Omaha experience, Moffat found time away from banking to buy and sell real estate. His efforts paid off, because by 1859, at age twenty and with escalating land values, he was a paper millionaire.[2] Despite the heady experience, he was still a minor and William Byers, who became a mentor and a lifelong friend, had to complete the paperwork until he left for Denver to begin his newspaper career as publisher of *The Rocky Mountain News.*

Moffat enjoyed Omaha and its frontier people. His charisma, initiative, and character brought him in contact with the right people. The earlier role models of a flock of aunts, uncles, cousins, parents, siblings, and grandparents had left their mark. He was soon in the social swirl and, although Omaha was a tiny town where it was easy enough to get shot, people living there or passing through had a better view of the Western potential. During his three years in Omaha, Moffat became close friends with George Kassler. Kassler would move on to Denver and an influential business career in water development. As mentioned, he also held a friendship with William Byers. Byers eventually left Omaha for Denver in April 1859 and endured six weeks of spring prairie storms and Indian attacks.

While in Omaha, Moffat established a friendship with the Woolworth brothers: C. C. Woolworth (probably Calvin Colton, 1833–1925) and C. D. Woolworth (probably Charles Dawson, 1837–?). Samuel Buel Woolworth (1800–1881) was their father. The brothers owned some book and stationery supply stores in various towns up and down the Missouri River. They were not the distant predecessors of Frank W. and Charles S. Woolworth, who formed the F. W. Woolworth retail chain in 1912. Furthermore, the 1860 St. Joseph, Missouri, city directory lists a C. C. and S. W. Woolworth. S. W. Woolworth may have been a son or another relative. The listing no longer existed after 1881. The 1860 and 1861 directory does list a C. C. and C. D. Woolworth and a business name of Woolworth and Colt (Benjamin F.) as booksellers and bookbinders. In 1871, the business was located at 83 Felix Street. The West often experienced boom and bust. In 1860, investment speculation fueled a bust that wiped out young Moffat's brief millionaire status. It was a sharp lesson and, after paying off his creditors, his character and bonds of friendship would hold up at a critical time as they would many times in the future.

The Woolworth brothers were interested in establishing a book and stationery supply store in Denver—and they favored Moffat with a position as manager. One source supports a partnership agreement: Woolworth and Moffat. In any event, three or four wagons loaded with books and stationery supplies and their drivers—along with Moffat—left Omaha on a cold February morning in 1860. The frigid trip took twenty-nine days, reaching Denver on March 17, 1860. The store was located across Cherry Creek at Auraria, now a three-college campus. The type of business was a good choice; the citizens were hungry for anything to read, and Moffat subscribed to some Eastern newspapers, which would arrive weekly by stage.

Moffat got on well in Denver just as he had in Omaha. The business grew, and he was able to secure enough capital to begin buying and shipping gold dust, later switching to more accurate bullion, which turned him a profit and more public exposure. Moffat was motivated by money. His personal ambition was to accumulate a personal fortune—$75,000 was one amount—and return home to

New York. Of course, thousands of other visitors to the West held similar visions.

The mining wealth pouring out of the nearby mountains and the economic activity elsewhere in Colorado were easy enough to see. However, slow-moving freight wagons—and even the faithful stagecoach with a ten-day run from Leavenworth and later Atchison, Kansas—would soon be incapable of supporting the growth that was taking place. A railroad—more than one—was needed. The Union Pacific was laying track from Omaha and the Kansas Pacific, which would cross central Kansas, was still readying itself at the Missouri River. The bookstore at Auraria was a success and, after a year, Moffat relocated back across Cherry Creek in the Post Office building at present day 14th and Larimer Streets. Moffat, in the meantime, was being noticed. At the close of 1861, he was appointed postmaster and a Western Union agent in 1862.

There was a more pressing issue, however. Leaving the business in good hands, he took the overland stage east to the Missouri River and the train to his former home in Washingtonville, New York, to marry Mary Frances Buckout. Their first home was in Auraria at 12th and Larimer Streets; they lived in a small house among the Indians who occupied the area long before Denver became a city. Their only child, Marcia, was born there.

In 1864, Moffat was appointed to serve as adjutant general for Colorado Territory. As the year ended, Moffat and his family experienced the threat and turmoil from the fallout of the November 1864 Sand Creek Battle (most people eventually agreed it was a massacre) during the height of the Indian wars of 1864–1866. He planned to take a family trip back East, but may have delayed with second thoughts about the dangers of the overland trip and even the security of Denver.

The Sand Creek Massacre was a tragic incident of misunderstandings and a stain on Colorado's citizens. There had been a series of isolated attacks on homesteaders and small wagon trains by rogue Indians. The attacks were brutal, with killings, burnings, and mutilations beyond the customary bounds of engagement. The final straw might have been the Hungate family massacre of the parents and their two daughters on their employer's ranch, southeast of Denver. In November 1864, a militia was formed with Colonel Chivington in command and the renegade Indians were tracked to their suspected location and attacked. Instead, the guilty Indians had left the camp and mostly innocent families were slain, while Chief Black Kettle flew the American flag of peace that had been given to him earlier in Denver. The policing event became a tragic murder party. Nevertheless, Moffat and his family left for the East in late 1865, returning safely to Denver in March 1866.

## Business Opportunities

Jerome B. Chaffee and Ebenezer Smith were early founders of the First National Bank of Denver, which was floundering. They approached Moffat to put the business on a sound footing. The failure of a bank just as Denver was finding its place on the map would be terrible. Moffat was appointed cashier on September 6, 1866.[4]

The position was just what Moffat had dreamed about—and was an opportunity to satisfy his dream of accumulating a personal fortune and triumphantly return to the East.

As he grew into the cashier position, Moffat found that he had a platform on which to exercise some of his financial ideas. Most of them turned out to be good ideas, including the eventual Moffat railroad project, which prospers today with the Moffat Tunnel as the key to the operation, although he never saw it fulfilled. The massive undertaking was simply more than one man and a few loyal investors could handle.

As the 1860s slid away, local railroading in Colorado was really getting started. There were plans to enter the mountains to reach the gold and silver camps—and Moffat was right in the middle of this Western development. He had naively hoped that the Union Pacific would make Denver a major location and cross the Rockies to the West, but by 1866, the Union Pacific had elected to remain north at Cheyenne to reach its Western destiny.

An incident at about the same time probably cemented their decision. General Grenville Dodge, the Union Pacific chief engineer—in an effort to accommodate the city of Denver and his employer—

ordered a survey party to try to locate a route over the mountains. Percy Brown was the on-site lead civil engineer and, with his party, they searched all summer and fall. Dodge decided to join the group and reached them in November—a risky time in the Colorado high country.

A sudden early winter blizzard struck with a severity so intense that the survey group, along with General Dodge, had to abandon their pack mules and survey equipment. Over a very long day-and-a-half march, they were barely able to make their way down into the Boulder Valley (present-day Boulder). Dodge's report to the Union Pacific board put an end to any speculation of a rail line over the Rockies.

Also, nearby Berthoud Pass from a prior survey would require an impossible three-and-a-half-mile tunnel, and it would be 2,000 feet higher than anything in Wyoming. Emotions were such that even the 104-mile connecting line to Cheyenne requested by Denver was denied until Denver investors funded the project.

## Business Profile

The local papers carried the Union Pacific remarks. It said, "Build the U. P. to Denver? No, indeed. Denver is too dead to bury." Denver didn't take the rebuff sitting down. In May 1868, a group of business leaders subscribed to a $300,000 bond issue to build the Denver Pacific Railroad and Telegraph Company to connect with the Union Pacific at Cheyenne. Moffat served as treasurer and the organization had several presidents, including General Bela M. Hughes, an attorney and earlier stagecoach figure with Ben Holladay, and W. F. Johnson, who died one month after his appointment. Governor John Evans finally saw the project to completion. Track laying went without incident; communities and businesses used the presence of the railroad to develop. The first engine from Cheyenne rolled into a jubilant Denver on June 24, 1870, carrying a David H. Moffat banner. Union Pacific officials must have viewed the connection in a reserved light, and Denver interests reportedly picked up most of the costs.

Moffat observed Denver's leaders, especially Governor John Evans. Evans was also a physician from Illinois who established the University of Denver and the Iliff School of Theology. As the railroad work progressed north from Denver and south from Cheyenne, Moffat jumped into the real estate opportunities. He may have played a minor part in the founding of Greeley, Colorado. New York editor Horace Greeley's "Go West" suggestion had an impact on a lot of impressionable people.

During the same time, the Kansas Pacific line—with some renewed financial assistance from the Union Pacific—struggled across Indian country while enduring one attack after another. It finally reached Denver on August 15, 1870. At some point, Moffat would call Denver his home for the remainder of his life.

Moffat was well aware that freight rates set by Eastern railroads discriminated against Colorado manufacturers and businesses. However, greater local opportunities were at hand. Moffat, John Evans, and Walter Cheesman, a real estate developer, partnered to build a local rail line to the shallow underground coal beds just to the north of Denver. Present-day Erie was selected to provide a reliable supply of locomotive fuel. The area is honeycombed with abandoned coal mines.

Prosperity continued; the 1870 census for Denver was 4,759 citizens. By 1890, it would be over 106,000. In 1871, the Moffat family was living in a larger home at 14th and Curtis Streets. In 1872, Moffat, Cheesman, Evans, and James Archer organized the Denver Water company—and the succeeding Union Water Company in 1890. Clean water was at a premium in growing Denver, and in 1880 Cheesman, then a druggist at 15th and Blake Streets, struck on the idea of bottling, selling, and even delivering water from some of the local artesian wells. Eleven water companies were formed and failed over a several-year period, but the Denver Union Water company started by Moffat, Evans, and Cheesman was a success. The same men went on to build Cheesman Dam on the South Platte southwest of Denver. It still delivers clean water to this day. The dam was completed in 1905 and for a time was the world's highest.

In 1872, Evans and Moffat organized the Denver and South Park Railroad. The route entered the mountains southwest of Denver at Morrison and ran from Morrison, up the Platte canyon and through the present-day locales of Kassler, Strontia Springs, Foxton, Buffalo

8

Creek, Bailey, Glenisle, Shawnee, Grant, and over Kenosha Pass below present-day US 285 into the vast two-mile-high South Park. The wagon and stage roads generally followed the railroad and are depicted in the Department of the Interior, United States Geological Survey Historic Trail Map, 1x2 degree Quadrangle, Central Colorado, 1999 by Glenn R. Scott, retired.

## Reaching South Park

The objective was to cross over Kenosha Pass at the eastern entrance of South Park and drive southwesterly about fifty miles across South Park first to Hartsel and then to Buena Vista and the Arkansas River. Then it was planned to lay track north to Leadville. The Denver and Rio Grande—led by William Palmer—was to move up from Colorado Springs through South Park, joining the Denver and South Park railroad at present-day Hartsel. The Denver and Rio Grande instead built into Leadville. The Denver and South Park Railroad expanded into the local mining camps and reached Leadville in 1896. The Denver and Rio Grande also advanced from Pueblo up the Arkansas River through the Royal Gorge past the earlier grief of the late 1860s and 1870s with the Santa Fe railroad. At Salida, the line would turn south over Poncha Pass into the San Luis Valley. The mineral wealth of the San Juan Mountains was directly to the west.

Rail lines were popping up—many near the front range. Boulder (City) wanted to have a railroad, and Moffat helped organize the Denver and Boulder Valley Railroad. For Moffat, it was one event after another in those heady days. In *The Switzerland Trail of America*, Forest Crossen depicts some of the local lines.

Leadville gained a second life when its discarded slag piles were reprocessed—and, by 1877, it was again growing. Moffat followed and purchased half interests in four mines, including H. A. W. Tabor's Little Pittsburg. The mine reportedly returned $100,000 monthly to Moffat over an undocumented period. It may have occurred. Mine profits in those days could be staggering. Tabor was the man who owned the Matchless Mine at Leadville; he later went on to become a United States senator and eventually plunged into bankruptcy after the silver panic that was triggered on April 22, 1893. The federal government wanted a gold standard and reduced the financial support for silver. Moffat went on to invest in the Caribou Mine in Boulder County and another mine at Cripple Creek until, according to public accounts, he owned or held an interest in one hundred mines around the state.

At one point, it is said that he confided to a friend that his wealth was $7 million. After his death in 1911, it was estimated that Moffat had actually directed nearly his entire fortune of $20 million into the railroad development. According to West Egg Inflation Calculator, $20 million is equivalent to $492,273,411 in today's values.

# CHAPTER 2:
# THE RIO GRANDE RAILROAD

S hortline railroads were beginning in Colorado, and General William J. Palmer's Rio Grande Railroad, with headquarters at Colorado Springs, was working to build a narrow gauge line from Pueblo up the Arkansas River Canyon. It would pass through the several-miles-long Royal Gorge to connect with Moffat's standard gauge at Salida.

Palmer was not alone in his endeavors. In *Railroads and the Rockies*, Robert Ormes uses an exhaustive 294-page index to document 1,328 railroad activities around Colorado and adjacent states during the late 1800s and early 1900s.

After a vicious territorial fight, the Rio Grande Railroad had overcome the Santa Fe threat to build along the Arkansas River and through the Royal Gorge. The Santa Fe temporarily retreated to southern Colorado. The defeat of the Santa Fe Railroad and the victory of General William Palmer's smaller, privately funded Rio Grande line at the Royal Gorge on the Arkansas River is a compelling story.[1]

Briefly, the Rio Grande was the first to survey Raton Pass between Trinidad in extreme southern Colorado and the later town of Raton, New Mexico, on the northern border. The objective was to develop the southwest area of the United States. The Santa Fe at some point followed with its own survey and the menacing intention of direct competition with the Rio Grande at any point where it might be running (mostly well to the north at the time). The Rio Grande people were beside themselves, and on February 26, 1868, Palmer decided to take a stand against William Strong, vice president and general manager of the Santa Fe.

The Arkansas River was considered the gateway to the central and southern mountain regions, and the river passed through the lengthy, narrow Royal Gorge and its thousand-foot chasm. Laying a railroad track alongside the river would be expensive and difficult.

By April, both lines had laid separate tracks nearly to the eastern mouth of Royal Gorge Canyon, but there would only be room for one set of tracks. There was as much spying going on as track laying— and a Rio Grande worker listening in on the telegraph line overheard that a party of Santa Fe people were about to make a dash for land above the Rio Grande workforce, which would place them in a key position. Palmer responded by ordering a hundred or so workers to begin construction work within the walls of the canyon.

Apparently aware that their plans had been discovered, the Santa Fe group sent one of its engines steaming north to Pueblo, and from there, an onboard survey engineer rode horseback. After his horse gave out, he continued on foot to Canon City. At the time, the population of Canon City was supposedly sympathetic to the Santa Fe cause after the earlier threats made by Palmer and his Rio Grande Railroad to extort $150,000 from nearby Pueblo before his line would stop there. It was hoped that the Santa Fe emissary could enlist a sufficient number of men in the Pueblo community to establish prior possession.

As the story goes, a half hour later, a group of Rio Grande men arrived and immediately detoured around the Santa Fe people. They advanced up the canyon for a few miles and either joined the first Rio Grande work group or moved beyond and immediately began grading. Emotions quickly rose to the boiling point, and men poured into each camp. With enough booze and guns, they were ready to fight—even though a day or two earlier many had been fellow workers, acquaintances, or friends. Palmer, in the meantime, turned to the courts and sought relief and an injunction against the Santa Fe with an eventual appeal to the US Supreme Court. Palmer and his smaller Denver and Rio Grande line were financially and emotionally drained by construction and legal costs. By 1878, he was forced to lease his line to the Santa Fe for thirty years. The terms of the lease contained an anti-discrimination clause prohibiting unfair freight rates.

Leadville, the silver capital, was booming and Palmer was able to free himself from Santa Fe matters at Pueblo and cross South Park from Colorado Springs and connect his line there with David Moffat's line, which now extended into Leadville. The two men never forgot their respect for each other.

The animosity between the Santa Fe and the Rio Grande remained despite the lease agreement, and by early 1879, Palmer discovered discriminating freight rates and neglect of the Rio Grande equipment. Sometime in March 1879, Palmer ordered a contingent of armed men to resume construction on the Arkansas-Royal Gorge leg. The Santa Fe workers, armed as well, were present in the area, and there was another wild jumping ahead by each group. For the historian who likes to see for himself, there is a scenic tourist train that operates into the Royal Gorge. Along the way, revetments for men and guns can still be seen.

Finally by April 2—a very long month—there was a rumor that the court would rule in favor of the Rio Grande. Despite some skirmishing from overheated participants, the Santa Fe was forced to withdraw. Palmer, applying a kind of scorched-earth policy, had his people seize all of the Santa Fe assets back down the line.

At Pueblo, the Santa Fe retrenched and recruited Bat Masterson, the famed and feared Dodge City sheriff. There, a group of men stood ready to fight any further push by the Rio Grande. Fortunately, cooler heads prevailed, and the line in the sand was never crossed. A court order ordered the Santa Fe property returned. Binding agreements were signed, identifying where each line could and could not build— and $1.4 million was awarded to the Santa Fe in settlement for the tracks already laid.

## Two Employers

After serving as cashier, Moffat was elected in 1880 to be president of the First National Bank of Denver, and he held the position until his death in 1911. Moffat sold his South Park railroad interests when he became president and invested in the Denver and New Orleans Railway, which later was renamed the Colorado and Southern. Over the years, Moffat would rely on assistance more than once from the Colorado and Southern. His family was also treated to its third home, at 1706 Lincoln Street. The fourth and final move was to a mansion at 808 Grant Street.

## Moffat and the Denver and Rio Grande

In 1880, Moffat's lifelong fascination with railroads prompted a board invitation from the Rio Grande line where he served on two successive boards before being elected president in 1885, serving until 1891. The line's earlier battle with the Santa Fe and the subsequent decision to reach the mining districts of the San Juan Mountains were monumental expenses, and the railroad was crippled. Nevertheless, the Rio Grande had to develop a profitable presence in the San Luis Valley. A direct route from Walsenburg and its coal fields was built over La Veta Pass at the southern part of the valley leading into the agricultural center at Alamosa. The San Luis Valley was proving to be an agricultural bounty. However, reaching the San Juan mountain range and the mining opportunities to the west was going to be expensive and difficult, but there was no alternative. The San Juan Mountains form a nearly impenetrable barrier. The company surveyors laid out a long, twisting route from the valley floor at Antonito and along the mountainous spine between Colorado and Chama, New Mexico. It became known as the Cumbres and Toltec leg. Today it operates as a scenic attraction.

Durango, at the southwest corner of Colorado, was the next objective, around seventy direct miles northwest. But there are no direct miles in that part of the country, and the surveyors had to chart another twisting course to Durango. The line extended generally northwest from Chama to Lumberton, Dulce, Navajo,

Tiffany, Ignacio, Oxford, Falfe, and Durango. (One local source had it westerly from Dulce to Farmington, New Mexico, to meet up with some short lines.)[3]

From Durango, it was another fifty-five or so miles north to present-day Silverton within the San Juan range. Most of the ore was then carried by rail over 400 miles back to smelters in Denver. Durango retained some smelting activity. Today, the scenic tourist line is known as the Durango-Silverton Railroad.

At the north entry to the valley, Poncha Pass, tracks were laid down the center of the valley and directly south to Alamosa, but the tracks have since been removed. There was a later spur to Del Norte. Today, the remainder of the valley has little railroad presence for the large area it serves.

David Moffat favored standard gauge rails because much greater loads could be carried, but he contended with narrow gauge when necessity chose. Actually, in 1883, the Denver and Rio Grande completed a narrow-gauge road into Salt Lake City. There were two operations at the time: The Denver and Rio Grande between Pueblo and Grand Junction and the Rio Grande Western between Grand Junction and Salt Lake City and Ogden, Utah, where there was a connection with the cautious Union Pacific. The Rio Grande business was a daily learning experience for Moffat—and he would need all of it within a few short years.

**Take-Over Action**

The dreaded event finally arrived in 1881. The Rio Grande and its leader, William Palmer, were financially exhausted and vulnerable. Jay Gould, the Eastern investor and railroad baron (some said predator), easily gained control and forced Palmer to leave the Rio Grande. Moffat was elected to the board in 1881, replacing David C. Dodge—Palmer's appointment. Gould apparently believed that Moffat would bring the right Western diversity to his board. Palmer, in turn, was replaced by Frederick Lovejoy as president, who then purged any remaining Palmer people.

Gould's tactics were relatively unsuccessful and, three years later, on July 12, 1884, the line was in receivership. William S. Jackson, the former Denver and Rio Grande treasurer, was appointed receiver. Lovejoy would be gone by February 25, 1885, and David H. Moffat was elected to the presidency at the same meeting of the directors in New York City. Jackson apparently managed well enough and the line emerged from bankruptcy on July 12, 1885. Moffat was faced with a new challenge to build the line through the narrow eleven miles of Glenwood Canyon and its towering thousand-foot walls reaching up from the Colorado River. Even the Native Americans were reportedly reluctant to enter the depths. Nevertheless, a rail bed was blasted out and tracks were laid. A jubilant Glenwood Springs at the western end was reached on October 5, 1887. A wagon and auto road would follow in 1905. Expansion opportunities were everywhere and, as mentioned earlier, a spur line was extended some forty-six miles east into Aspen from Glenwood Springs and thirty-seven miles south from Montrose to Ouray at the northern boundary of the San Juan Mountains.

For several years, Moffat served concurrently as president of the First National Bank and the Denver and Rio Grande Railroad. In a novel manner, he would divide his day between each office. As the 1880s closed, both organizations were able to post some profitable returns. Moffat had come a long way in the thirty or so years after he first arrived in Denver.

Moffat and his people were searching for a direct route to Salt Lake City, but so were other railroad interests. The only route at the time was west from Pueblo, one hundred miles south of Denver, continuing through Royal Gorge Canyon and on to Grand Junction, and terminating at Salt Lake City-Ogden, Utah. The road passed through the Gunnison, Montrose, and Delta communities and generally followed present-day US Highway 50. Some stretches of the route were difficult and impractical to operate and costly to maintain. Even in recent years, the route was indirect and dangerous—and a lot of freight revenue was being lost to delay and expenses. Still, the company relied on the route and the alternative Leadville branch (a steep, twisting shortcut) until recent years when both were finally discontinued by the operating Union Pacific because of accidents and upkeep. Moffat used his authority to expand and improve the roads, but it was a contest with the board members who were hesitant to change.

The Burlington Railroad always seemed to be surveying something. From 1884 until 1887, it was to locate still better road locations—maybe a shortcut. Several years earlier, the Burlington—a Midwestern line that had ventured west—joined with the Colorado Midland to build a line beyond Leadville at 10,000 foot elevation. The early tracks would go over Tennessee Pass and through the Hagerman Tunnel (collapsed early on and never rebuilt) down to the Eagle River, which joined the Colorado River at Dotsero Junction on present day I-70. The subsequent alternative road was little better and went from Leadville to the molybdenum mine at Climax and then followed a steep, twisting descent past present-day Minturn to the Eagle River and on to Dotsero at the Colorado River. The Burlington ownership of parts of the route would eventually play a major influence.

The original Moffat route to Salt Lake City never changed to any extent. The forty-one-mile Dotsero Cutoff was still a survey point. From the west side of Rollins Pass at Winter Park, the road continued past the Tabernash repair shops and marshalling yard, then ten or so miles to Granby; Hot Sulphur Springs; Byers Canyon (known then as Yarmony); tiny Parshall, and Kremmling. The Colorado River and railroad were joined in the narrow Byers and Gore Canyons before reaching State Bridge, Bond, and McCoy. From there, the route would snake along to Steamboat Springs and Hayden, reaching Craig at the northwestern corner of the state in 1913 and over two hundred miles from Denver. Moffat may not have been aware of the geology of the Colorado River and how it favored the eventual Dotsero route. The northwest direction to Salt Lake seemed locked in his mind—perhaps understandably so given what he had been through with Harriman and the Union Pacific.

**Nature Presides**

Over the ages, the forces of nature formed a better route to transit west-central Colorado. At McCoy, the Colorado River flows southwest past the hamlets of Burns and Dotsero (meaning dot zero, a surveying term) and present day I-70. The forty-one-mile leg is an easy 1.5

percent grade depicted in Griswold's Denver Northwestern and Pacific Railroad. After Dotsero, the river enters the dark interior of Glenwood Canyon. This "Dotsero Cutoff" provided a huge assist to any railroad interests and the right-of-ways were surveyed over and over, purchased, sold, and argued in courts for years. Today, it is the Colorado mainline for the Union Pacific and Amtrak to Salt Lake City and beyond. The 1880s Dotsero Cutoff would also define the ultimate limits of the Moffat line during its construction. One might think that with Moffat's Denver and Rio Grande board member and president experience, he would have followed the present-day route rather than into northwestern Colorado. He simply wanted his own line. Also, the legal impediments of right-of-ways, financing, and the fact that his former employer—the Denver and Rio Grande—was a competitor in 1902 and held some easements at Dotsero may have had an influence. However, the Moffat people also retained a key Dotsero easement, described later, which the Rio Grande had to deal with. Also, Moffat may have correctly believed he held the trump card with the only direct route out of Denver—and his dream of the tunnel through the Continental Divide, which did not become absolutely true until 1928, seventeen years after his death.

While president of the Denver and Rio Grande, Moffat was able to resist the aggressive legal maneuvers of the other lines while the Denver and Rio Grande shrewdly purchased the stretch of the Burlington-Midland road from Leadville into Glenwood Springs, including the Dotsero Cutoff.

The Union Pacific president, E. H. Harriman, continued to regard Moffat as a threat and kept a close watch on what was taking place in Colorado. His Union Pacific line swept through long, unbroken stretches across Nebraska and Wyoming, connecting in Ogden with the Central Pacific, which ran its route between the vast Utah-Nevada interior and California. The Union Pacific route was profitable because Harriman had made it so after rescuing the company from years of neglect, fraud, huge construction debts, and a downward spiral following the May 10, 1869, transcontinental connection at Promontory Point, Utah. With completion of the transcontinental connection, freight and passenger traffic was projected to boom.

The immediate reality was that the revenue was marginal and could not support the construction debts and mismanagement. Moreover, Congress regarded some of the federal assistance to the two railroads as a loan. Harriman was a focused person and was obsessed with any real or perceived threat to his line. Within a few years, he would also control the Southern Pacific Railroad.

To the south, the Santa Fe (Atchison-Topeka) line was struggling across the southwestern landscape, reaching Los Angeles in 1880, but this was of little or no interest to Moffat. His nagging concern was that the objectives of the Rio Grande Railroad board were simply different from his, and he continued to search for another railroad opportunity.

Despite Moffat's growing objections and discontent over wasted efforts and money, the Rio Grande continued building west and into Grand Junction. From there, it reached northwest across Utah to join the Union Pacific in Ogden.

During the railroad experience, Moffat was still a banker and investor—and he greatly increased his wealth by investing in mining. The Silver Panic of 1893 struck hard in Colorado, and the First National Bank was threatened like the rest. Moffat reportedly advanced $2 million of his own money to shore up the bank, an action that had a positive impact on the other banks around the state.

The year of decision was 1891. Later that year, he resigned from the Rio Grande. The luster of the job was lost with the business direction the railroad was taking. The discovery of gold at Creede in 1891 was a big event. Moffat saw an opportunity to build a line into the area, but the proposal was voted down by the board and distant investors. Moffat responded by building his own spur line—and he repeated the same thing into Cripple Creek. Both lines were soon prospering and quickly purchased by the Rio Grande. At Glenwood Springs, Moffat pushed the successful spur line up the Roaring Fork Valley into Aspen.

# CHAPTER 3:

## CROSSROADS

F undamentally, Moffat wanted his own railroad, and the time finally arrived in 1902. Incorporation papers were filed on July 18, 1902, for the Denver, Northwestern, and Pacific Railroad Company. The incorporators were David H. Moffat, Walter S. Cheesman, William J. Evans, Charles J. Hughes Jr., George E. Ross-Lewin, Samuel M. Perry, and Frank B. Gibson. The company officers were Moffat, president, W. J. Evans, vice-president, F. B. Gibson, secretary, and Thomas Keely, treasurer. There were seven directors from the overall group. Moreover, the operation never enjoyed a wide array of investors.

Moffat, age sixty-three, pledged $4 million of his own bonds to the project (later an estimated $20 million would flow out of his estate). By 1903, the annual payroll had reached $400,000. Commercial operations would begin on June 23, 1904, when the first train crept over Rollins Pass crowned by the 11,660-foot-elevation Corona facilities. Operations continued until April 30, 1913, when the line would be sold at foreclosure. Moffat had died two years earlier, and the Denver and Salt Lake Railroad, a new owner, would take control on May 1, 1913. In 1912, the Denver, Utah, and Pacific Railroad and the Denver-Salt Lake line briefly merged. The Denver and Rio Grande and the Denver and Salt Lake lines concluded the turbulent era with a final merger in 1947.[1]

The steam-powered railroad line was nearly derailed at the outset. Moffat owned a one-half interest with William G. Evans in the Denver Tramway Company or, more formally, the Denver Northwestern Electric Company. Evans was also vice president in the Moffat operation. The two had apparently discussed the feasibility of an electric-powered train, but while Evans was in New York seeking investor funds, Moffat must have had second thoughts and wired Evans that he was going ahead with a steam railroad to Salt Lake City as planned.

Many years earlier—during the 1870s—Denver officials had exercised considerable efforts to locate a suitable location for roads that would safely and profitably accommodate travel and commerce into the western interior of Colorado.

Thirty-seven years later, in 1902, Moffat and his associates set out on a direct route west to Salt Lake City; it would be over and through the Rockies, saving about 175 miles. The distance might seem trivial, but 175 miles meant a lot of potential freight revenue. The route would be an opening to the wealth of the western interior of Colorado and lower freight charges to Salt Lake City, which had been a hub to the West Coast and a strategic location since its founding.

# CHAPTER 4:
## FRIEND AND FOE

The first order of business for Moffat was to secure financing. As a banker, he believed he knew something about financing, but he was in for a surprise. He was surely aware of the cold hostility from the several men who controlled the major railroads. James J. Hill, president of the Great Northern between St. Paul and Puget Sound; Edward Henry Harriman Jr., president of the Union Pacific and eventually the Southern Pacific; and Jay Gould, a keen and skilled investor (some said unscrupulous) with a former interest in the Rio Grande and the Burlington (and a dozen other railroads). There may have been others, but the three kingmakers were visibly angered that Moffat had not sought their approval before building his railroad. The group retaliated by coercing Wall Street banking interests to withhold any investment support for Moffat, which, of course, left Moffat and his few local investors on their own. Not one of the three could see a chance for success.[1]

General William J. Palmer (1836–1909), a kind of patron saint to present-day Colorado Springs, was one of the architects of the Rio Grande Railroad. Immediately prior to his Rio Grande connection, Palmer was manager of construction during the completion of the Kansas Pacific's final 240-mile leg from Sheridan, Kansas, into Denver, arriving there in August 1870. The stage lines, to accommodate the inevitability of their eventual demise, would run their closing days with a slightly shorter trip each week as the railroad tracks advanced. Eventually, the Union Pacific would absorb the Kansas Pacific line. Years later, a succession of lines would operate over the old road across Kansas and eastern Colorado (present-day US 40).

The Santa Fe Railroad, well to the south, built its road along the Santa Fe Trail up to Trinidad at the foot of Raton Pass, which separates Colorado and New Mexico. Surveys of the pass were made just as the Rio Grande had done, but now the Santa Fe turned north to Pueblo, reaching a cheering crowd in 1876. General Palmer's problems were just beginning, including the later destructive influence of Jay Gould.

In 1871, Palmer had planned on Colorado City being his Rio Grande Railroad headquarters. The community was between the adjacent mountains and Colorado Springs, but land prices were higher and Palmer opted for Colorado Springs, which was formally founded by the general on July 31, 1871. Palmer approached Pueblo, thirty-five miles south, whose citizens were still thrilled with train service from anywhere, and presented an ultimatum that Pueblo must raise a $150,000 subscription, or the Rio Grande would bypass Pueblo. What few friends Palmer and his railroad might have had were now firmly in the Santa Fe camp. The Denver Rio Grande eventually delivered service to Pueblo in 1872.

General Grenville Mullen Dodge (1831–1916) was never hostile to Moffat and his group, although he worked for the Union Pacific and President Harriman. Later he joined the Santa Fe as a chief civil engineer. There is some reference that Dodge had been involved in lobbying citizens in the towns along the road that the railroads would pass through to encourage their support. The practice at the time was apparently not that uncommon, but eventually there were accusations of misappropriation of some of the money when the Crédit Mobilier scandal broke. The lobbying activity involved financial contributions to Congress, and Dodge—among others—was summoned to appear before a committee. He chose to hide and never did appear.

When Union Pacific was founded 1863, the Crédit Mobilier Corporation of America was organized at about the same period to facilitate the construction of public works.

The Union Pacific—even at the height of the Civil War—never was profitable, but it was the only line between the Missouri River and the Pacific as late as 1873. Building 1,300 miles of railroad across a virtual wilderness could not be done without federal help. At completion, there was still a $13 million debt for the Union Pacific; the Central Pacific had similar problems.

The Pacific Railroad Act of 1862 and 1864 provided considerable relief through land grants of alternate 640-acre sections per mile and outright loans of subsidy bonds after each twenty miles of laid track. Furthermore, the government issued second mortgage bonds, which permitted each railroad line to reissue as first mortgage bonds to investors.

The Crédit Mobilier investment plan turned out to be very profitable, yet the railroad still ran short of money. In the meantime, the threat of a Congressional investigation was at hand. Oakes Ames, Crédit Mobilier's president, decided to issue 343 shares of Crédit Mobilier stock to selected members of Congress and some other government officials. The transaction was to be transparent and not intended in any way to be free. The recipients were expected to pay for the stock. One distribution method suggested was through the expected dividend stream from the stock. The stock was doing well and reportedly would increase in value by 500 percent of its original price.[2]

**Crédit Mobilier Investigation**

When the Union Pacific was founded in 1863, the Crédit Mobilier Corporation of America was organized at about the same period to better facilitate the construction of public works. America was bursting with energy for public growth, and the Mobilier Corporation was an instant success. In 1867, Union Pacific thought enough of the company to buy up the majority of the stock and increased the working capital to $3,750,000. Soon extraordinary dividends were being paid, while the value of the company was soaring. It was inevitable that public opinion would turn suspicious and become further directed when it was revealed that certain members of Congress were principal shareholders. The ensuing scattered scandals and accusations dampened public opinion of Congress. Dodge may have been distant from any serious charges and the matter appeared to be dropped.

Dodge was born in Danvers, Massachusetts, and educated as a civil engineer. He relocated with his family to Council Bluffs, Iowa, on the east bank of the Missouri River and always referred to the place as his home. During the Civil War, he served in the Union Army, reaching the rank of brigadier general and was wounded twice. After the war, he was posted for a year at nearby Fort Leavenworth, where—with a tiny contingent of troops and equipment—he was responsible for the security of the open frontier between eastern Kansas and Denver, over 600 miles to the west.

During his youth, Dodge was probably no different from other young men. His first job away from family influence was with a section crew laying railroad tracks. That rigor may have influenced him at some point to obtain a formal education as a surveyor and civil engineer. The survey party he was part of was reportedly responsible for the 1860 survey of the Union Pacific Railroad line from Omaha to Salt Lake City—a monumental achievement.

Thomas Durant, Union Pacific's president before Harriman, hired Dodge in 1869 as the transcontinental connection was nearing completion to oversee the land department, which was rapidly growing with all of the accruing government benefits and liabilities. Sometime during his Union Pacific employment between 1869 and 1870, Grenville Dodge was part of the near-fatal November surveying party in the Colorado Mountains' mentioned earlier.

Dodge made a career change, and in 1871, he was appointed the chief engineer for the Santa Fe line as it was built across southern Kansas and southeastern Colorado. His immediate superior, Thomas A. Scott, wanted to complete what the stage lines did with their early routes between San Antonio, El Paso, and California. The stage lines had even established connecting points on the Gulf Coast and New Orleans for steamboat travel on the Mississippi River and rail travel to the Atlantic Coast. For the stagecoach lines, the travel between connections was endless—and it was simply too much. In any event, the Santa Fe eventually reached a welcoming Los Angeles in 1880.

Jay Gould (1836–1892) was never a railroad man in the sense of simply operating a line. He was a financier in predatory terms, which wasn't that different from what others were doing—Gould was simply better at it. For Gould, financial control was a science and he was absolutely among the best. After the 1869 transcontinental connection, the Union Pacific languished with a $13-million debt, which grew to $75 million. Congress demanded some repayment as part of the earlier bargain. The railroads of course disagreed, and the ongoing controversy during 1877 and 1878 finally influenced Gould to leave the board. Moreover, the Union Pacific directors were derelict in their stewardship, leaving a history of costly loans to themselves.[3]

Gould first acquired a financial interest in the Union Pacific in 1873 when he was able to purchase from Thomas Scott, a Southern Pacific official, 100,000 shares and a seat on the board. Gould had reportedly lost interest in the manipulation of the Eastern railroads, and the lengthy Union Pacific promised a challenge. He worked at restoring the railroad to a profitable footing and was elected president in March 1874. Wall Street reacted with the expectation that Gould would raid the Union Pacific assets and then leave the line in ruins, but Gould had different intentions.

During his tenure with Union Pacific, Gould found another opportunity right under his nose. In 1875, Gould wanted to control the tiny forty-eight-mile Panama Railroad that was completed in 1854 to operate across the isthmus between the Atlantic and Pacific Oceans. It became a contest between Gould and his adversary, Collis P. Huntington, president of the Southern Pacific Railroad. The prize was the Pacific Mail steamship line, which carried mail, cargo, and passengers between Panama and San Francisco.

The Panama steamship line carried the same between Panama, New Orleans, other Gulf ports, and New York. Neither line was particularly profitable, partly due to postmaster cost controls. A competing line was even organized—the Occidental and Oriental—but it was never activated. The overland stagecoach lines demonstrated by 1865 that they could carry important mail between Washington and California as fast as—or often faster—than the steamship lines. Heavy cargo of course would remain with the ships and the transcontinental railroad after 1869.

However, what had been overlooked by at least some people was the "China Trade," the potential Asian market. The traditional Eastern trade routes had been by clipper ships around Cape Horn. Thousands of miles and months of travel could be eliminated by a forty-eight-mile railroad. A ship canal across the isthmus had been discussed for years, but this would be well into the future. The trade idea never caught on to any appreciable extent. Those who wanted to trade did so, but there was never a mass movement until completion of the Panama Canal. Prior to Panama, an overland crossing was used at Tegucigalpa, Honduras.

Gould's presence had an influence on Union Pacific; its shares climbed from $15 in November 1873 to $78 in March 1875. As early as 1868–1869, Union Pacific found itself in the coal business, partly because of the earlier land grants. By 1874, management originated a plan to begin its own coal mining and coal transportation, which continues to this day. Gould even found himself in the unlikely scenario of dealing with Thomas Edison by virtue of Gould's investment in Western Union and his subsequent turn to Atlantic and Pacific Telegraph stock when he found Edison was not overly responsive to Gould's objectives.

While still on the board during 1873 and prior to being elected president in 1874, Gould wanted the Kansas Pacific to be a Union Pacific subsidiary, and the Denver-Cheyenne railroad, started by Denver investors, to be consolidated. He reasoned that the Union Pacific stock would be worth more. Gould held controlling interest in the two lines, but the Union Pacific board closed ranks and Gould was left with two failing lines, although the 104-mile Denver-Cheyenne road should have been profitable.

During 1873, an angry Gould bundled together some of his smaller Midwestern lines that were doing little and threatened the board that he would fashion a competing railroad to the Pacific and one to the Gulf Coast. The Railroad Act of 1862 mandated that branch lines operate as one line, and Union Pacific management relented and purchased both lines. During the episode, the public got wind of the conflict, and Gould's Union Pacific stock zoomed to reportedly $10 million. Emerging from the icy storm in the board room, Gould would be elected president the following year.

Gould employed a methodical financial system. He apparently focused on how he might manipulate the securities of a company, believing that the true wealth of a company was in its securities. Jay Gould started life with little, but his first success was surveying and making some maps for investors and local communities. His work was regarded as good, and with this success, he moved on to the leather tanning business, where with considerable self-discipline he succeeded. Eventually, he got into the stock market as a broker. His personal fiber was energy, intellect, cold reasoning, and a virtual absence of normally accepted ethical qualities. Gould, on the other hand, believed that his personal guidelines were rules that all should be able to operate under. He simply lived in his own world. He was not particularly well liked, was good to his family, and died in 1892 at a relatively young age of fifty-six as a very wealthy man. The official count was $77 million.[4]

Edward (E. H.) Harriman Jr., was a board member in 1897 and elected chairman of the Union Pacific executive committee in 1898, and essentially he had the final say in Union Pacific matters. He may have taken the joint title of president at some point. Harriman was the principal opponent of Moffat until his death in 1909 in New York City. Harriman was born February 25, 1848, in Washingtonville, New York, which is the same small close-knit community where Moffat grew up—and where the source of contentions may have originated. Both families have very long and honorable histories. The Harriman family immigrated to the Washingtonville area from England in June 1795. William Harriman, the family leader and Edward Henry Harriman Jr.'s great-grandfather, did not arrive penniless as the American success stories have a wont to go. The elder Harriman was reportedly a successful stationery merchant in London and—like the Moffats—was one of a few English citizens at the time that held favorable views of the American colonists and may have supported their objectives.[5]

After William Senior, there was Edward and Orlando Harriman

Jr. Orlando Jr. was Edward Harriman Jr.'s father, and he chose the ministry over family business. Rural America in the mid-1800s was a defining prospect for a pastor. Income from a country church was virtually nothing, and with a growing family, Reverend Orlando received a call in 1850 to travel to the new state of California and minister to those in the gold rush. Leaving that May by steamer to Panama, he struggled across the steamy isthmus along with his fellow passengers to the Pacific side and a waiting steamer. The convenience of a railroad would not be available for another four years, so walking, horseback, and canoe transportation were the best available. After a month of travel, Reverend Harriman, suffering from tropical fever, reached San Francisco and promptly left for the gold fields and the source of his pastor's call. Unfortunately, the position had been filled by a new Episcopal rector; the trustees thought Harriman had decided not to come. Harriman, no doubt in a desperate condition, found whatever work he could and preached whenever the opportunity was offered. The eleven months in California and the harsh life in the gold fields was a test of resolve, which he met. The following April, the plucky minister returned to the East Coast and settled his family in Jersey City, New Jersey.

Edward Henry Harriman Jr., no doubt seeking more worldly effects than his family had to offer, left home and school at fourteen and went to work at the New York Stock Exchange as a messenger. He must have been adept because he advanced to what was then the trusted position of carrying buy-and-sell orders between the exchange and its customers. In 1870 at age twenty, Harriman, with $3,000 in borrowed funds from an uncle, bought his own seat on the exchange. One of his early customers was Jay Gould, a man destined to rain havoc on Harriman in his later Union Pacific years.

The 1880s were big railroad times in the United States, and Harriman was losing interest in the stock market. A few years earlier—from 1877–1888—he had owned and operated a river steamboat that serviced the Hudson River commerce. His first railroad opportunity arrived in 1881 when, along with some investors, he purchased the nearly bankrupt Lake Ontario and Southern line and all of its thirty-four miles of track. The railroad, however, was located in such a manner that the nearby New York Central and the Pennsylvania line suddenly discovered that the thirty-four miles of rusty track was the ideal property to connect with the Great Lake ports and their inland tracks. Young Harriman's business skills and perceptions were keen. He cleaned up his railroad and rebuilt whatever was necessary—and then, after buying out most of his investors, he created a bidding war between the boards of the two competing giants with the Pennsylvania finally winning.

Generally, Harriman employed a basic business operation in his conquests: gaining control through sale of low-interest bonds to leverage assets, reorganization, expansion, and profit taking. In 1883, Harriman held enough Illinois Central stock that he was elected to the board and appointed vice president in 1887. He also purchased the Southern Pacific stock and enough Central Pacific Railroad stock held by Collis P. Huntington to gain control. Harriman tried to gain control of the Burlington and Quincy—serving the Chicago markets—but was turned away by James J. Hill and his Great Northern Railroad. By then, he had accumulated enough enemies and criticism to remain with him for the rest of his life. Harriman's son, William Averell Harriman, would go on to become a twentieth-century statesman and ambassador.

E. H. Harriman, as he was known during his business career, was recognized as the leader who rescued the Union Pacific, which was losing money. He was able to secure a board appointment in 1877, which probably came with the influential backing of the Standard Oil Company (Henry Rogers, William Rockefeller, and James Stillman). Harriman paid off the $75-million Union Pacific debt and, from 1900–1910, revenues rose by 90 percent. He also restored the Central Pacific to profitability and gained control of the Southern Pacific.

## Other Big Names

James J. Hill, known as the Empire Builder, built the Great Northern Railroad and never seemed to be particularly hesitant about his accomplishments. His biography is not materially different from the hard-driving leaders of the time. In *James J. Hill: Empire Builder of the West*, he was recognized as an astute, ambitious young man who started with little personal wealth, and his driving ambitions probably came at a cost to others.

Hill was born near Rockwood, Ontario, in 1838 and lived until 1916. His career path followed the other men who would be tomorrow's leaders. In 1854, at age sixteen, he was working on a steamboat traveling the Mississippi River, and in 1865, he was a freight agent. He eventually would own his own steamboat line.

At some point, the bankrupt St. Paul and Winnipeg Railroad caught his attention as something he could manage. With three other investors, he was able to seize control and—over fifteen years—build the line into a profitable operation. From the success of the St. Paul and Winnipeg line, Hill built the Great Northern Railroad. As one might expect, Hill had the capacity to inspire those around him and alienate an equal number. He was regarded as a raging autocrat and he could turn a blind eye toward an ethical situation. Hill eventually relocated to St. Paul, Minnesota. One remarkable characteristic shared by all of these nineteenth century business leaders was that each of them early on mastered the elements of their careers: vision, energy, ambition, and drive. Primarily, though, they knew virtually everything about their businesses.

J. P. Morgan invested in Hill's railroad in 1895, and although Hill needed the financial boost, he resented the strict controls that the Morgan bankers placed on his management style. In the fall of 1898, a falling out nearly occurred until Morgan relented and agreed that Hill knew more about the railroad business than he did. Morgan released Hill from the control of the Morgan voting trust, and he was able to operate his two railroads as independent operations.

Hill pushed on investing in iron mining, shipping, and a wide range of investments—most with the view as to where his railroad would benefit. The Red River Valley from North Dakota into Winnipeg, Canada, was a huge granary (and still is), which Hill and his railroad helped develop. He was instrumental in encouraging Scandinavian immigrants to settle in the Dakotas and Minnesota. Great Northern struggled across the northern Dakota and on to the Pacific Northwest after some lean years, including a seven-year hiatus on the banks of the Missouri River at Bismarck, North Dakota.

Hill and Harriman first came into conflict when both of them were trying to buy Chicago Burlington and Quincy stock. Harriman wanted more control of the Burlington and went about it by buying Northern Pacific stock and eventually held a majority of shares. Hill took exception and viewed Harriman as a primary adversary who had sneaked in under the fence. At about the same time, he learned that a David Moffat out in Colorado was trying to secure financing to establish a railroad through the Rocky Mountains and into Salt Lake City. His anger was first at Harriman and then at this Moffat person. Few on Wall Street were going to go up against the Harriman-Hill duo, which was difficult for Moffat searching for financing. A few years later, Hill, Harriman, and Morgan set their differences aside to form the Northern Securities Company, a holding company to prevent railroad competition. In 1904, the Supreme Court dissolved the entity. James Hill's closing years made the Northern Pacific a success for the northern tier of the country with first-class service.

Former bank officers Eugene H. Adams and Lyle W. Dorsett, and former vice president and historian Robert S. Pulcipher, provide a chronology in the unpublished *The Pioneer Western Bank: The First of Denver* (The First National Bank of Denver, N. A. and the First Interstate Bank of Denver, 1984.) The State Historical Society of Colorado serves as an additional depository of historical bank records. Robert Pulcipher, it might be added, researched and authored in 1971 an in-depth history in the form of a thesis of the First National Bank of Denver and its officers and directors from 1858–1915.

David Moffat spent nearly fifty years with the bank, which served as a critical linchpin in the financing of his railroad career. From a historical view, brothers Milton and Austin Clark and Emanuel Gruber, after founding their first bank at Leavenworth, Kansas Territory, in 1859—and no doubt flushed with success—moved to Denver and opened their doors on July 10, 1860, as Clark Gruber and Company Bank and Mint. At the time, Congress sanctioned the dual activity of assaying, minting gold coins, and commercial banking until 1863 when a US mint was authorized, and the Clark Gruber equipment sold to the government. The Clark Gruber banking operation was then merged with the First National Bank of Denver.

The Denver Mint was a welcome presence despite the profitable operation of minting coins. Assaying is a critical function—today and then—when a business deal was often sealed with a pinch or more of gold dust. However, there were inherent errors of just what constituted a "pinch" and the quality of the gold. It varies from location to location, often resulting in surprises.

With the mint matter completed, Clark-Gruber, with some investors, applied to the Comptroller of the Treasury for a charter for the First National Bank of Colorado. David Moffat, Henry J. Rogers, Governor John Evans, Jerome Chaffee, Ebenezer Smith, and others pushed the legislation forward despite Congressional dithering. The request was set aside until 1864. Finally, a charter was issued for Denver—not Colorado—on March 9, 1865. The bank opened its doors on May 10.[10] Jerome Chaffee and Ebenezer Smith were the principal officers. George T. Clark was the cashier. David Moffat would be the second cashier.

From the get-go, the bank worked at obtaining Eastern and European investors and depositors. Capital was in short supply on the Western Frontier, and the financing of heavy and costly mining equipment was essential; otherwise the mining boom for Colorado would be reduced to simple panning beside a streambed or the destructive hydraulic mining. The loan diversification was indeed broad. A notable customer during the 1870s was Charles Goodnight and the Charles Goodnight Ranch and the epic cattle drives. From this beginning, David Moffat began to accumulate his wealth. In the meantime, Denver's population had soared from 5,000 in 1870 to over 35,000 in 1880. By 1880, Colorado's population had reached 194,327.[12]

**The Moffat Regime 1880–1911**

After the 1880 retirement of President Jerome B. Chaffee, David Moffat was elected president. Until his death in 1911, he would preside over the First National Bank and the Denver and Rio Grande Railroad. After his resignation from the Rio Grande, it would be David Moffat's railroad: the Denver, Northwestern, and Pacific Railroad.

During this period of rapid national and bank growth, the Silver Panic of 1893, the slow return to the gold standard, and numerous bank failures, Moffat relied on an uncanny understanding of the economy and his two financial engines. He also understood mineral development, and it helped make him very wealthy.

Unlike many banks at the time, the First National was able to make large and small loans as the state economy grew.

As the Moffat Line grew from its 1902 start, so did the operating expenses, which were largely funded at the outset by Moffat. At the height of his operations—winter was the worst—they eventually consumed 41 percent of the line's revenue. Even after reaching the rich coal deposits in Routt County, expenses gutted the revenue. Also, despite the favorable audit reports by the comptroller over the years, Moffat gradually squeezed the bank as his own funds and the bank loans were slowly being crushed together. Moffat was not reckless—in his view—but the numbers were there. In 1909, Moffat remarked that he might be worth $8 million; after an audit, the comptroller suggested $10 million. After his death, the original estate was valued at some $20 million.

# CHAPTER 5:
## GETTING STARTED

T he first survey contracts to determine where the tracks would be located were awarded on December 18, 1902, to Orman and Crook of Pueblo, Colorado, and George L. Good and Company of Lockhaven, Pennsylvania. The first construction contract was issued to the Denver-Utah Construction Company. Sylvester T. Smith was the president. The line would pass by Coal Creek Canyon and advance up South Boulder Creek Canyon, northwest of Denver. Twenty-eight to thirty tunnels were anticipated—thirty-three would be the final count as the rail bed was blasted out and steel rails laid first along South Boulder Creek and finally over Rollins Pass.

With the aid of a relatively new tool, a Roberts track-laying machine, the crews were able to lay about one mile each day. The fall of 1902 and all of 1903 was a busy time as surveyors and engineers scrambled to get a sense of where they were going. Rail beds were prepared, tunnels were blasted out, bridges were built over streams, and trestles—some clinging to cliffs—were erected on both sides of the mountain canyons. The event was a continuous on-the-edge experience.

The first work engine nosed up the canyon in 1902; shortly thereafter, winter arrived with a fury. Snow removal became an emergency, and more than three hundred men were reportedly hired off the streets of Denver to shovel snow above 9,000 feet as the snow sheds were being constructed to keep the tracks clear for the construction trains.

With this intense type of an operation, accidents were inevitable. Within the first few days, there was one death and one loss of sight. The accidents never really let up over the years—to man and machine—despite unusual employee loyalty.

The line northwest out of Denver is largely unchanged from the original surveys. Utah Junction at the north end of the present-day Denver yards remains as the first transit point. The Moffat organization inherited a decrepit roundhouse, which they shored up, and they went on to build a repair depot and rail yards.

Leyden Junction was the next key location (it was first an underground coal mine and later a natural gas storage facility. Today it is a water reservoir). At Pinecliffe, a relatively level, 2 percent roadbed extends for several miles up to Tolland after a seemingly endless twisting climb through a series of costly tunnels. Tolland, originally called Mammoth, lies at the east base of James Peak. The location served as a communications center between Denver and the mountains. Today, one can drive near the old area. A few old cabins gaze back with stories of Western yesterdays.

The Moffat organization prided itself on the fact that, throughout its history, no passenger lives were ever lost, which was a considerable statement, given the risks of mountain railroading. A higher wage base at $3.43 per day was regarded as a premium for those who worked up on the pass, compared to the $2.00 per day paid for less rigorous labor elsewhere on the line.

The original plans had been to build a tunnel at the outset—to get the objective over and done with—but that immediately fell through when the anticipated financing from Wall Street never materialized. Instead, the alternative plan became the immediate plan as work on Rollins Pass went ahead as though it had always been intended.

One of Moffat's wisest decisions was to hire H. A. Sumner as his chief engineer, and Sumner loyally supported Moffat throughout the project. Carl Ridgeway was appointed construction superintendent and later was general manager.

**Achievement**

On June 23, 1904, the first passenger train carefully moved across the last trestle and into the safety of the partially completed snow shed at the top of the pass at Corona, 11,660 feet above sea level. From Corona, the tracks went down to Arrow, reaching there on September 18, seventy-six miles west of Denver and the charm of another world. Stagecoaches carried the passengers from Arrow onto the Western Slope and the wonder of the Western Frontier. On September 2, 1904, the first local freight service took place. Arrow would serve as a major division point during the entire Rollins Pass era. The location was also an assembly center for cattle shipping, logging, and lumber for Eastern shipments. The Arrow location was given the name because the wye used to turn a locomotive in the opposite direction resembled an arrowhead. For a while, it was known as Arrowhead, but it was later shortened to Arrow. The place had eating, drinking, and sleeping quarters, some stores, and loading facilities for lumber, logs, and livestock. There was even a small cemetery now hidden within the forest. Today, Arrow, nearly forgotten, lies on a bluff above Winter Park ski resort.

The other lines—local and national—knew exactly what was taking place. Those who perceived an economic threat attacked Moffat at every opportunity. Moffat's view was that he was attempting to do what none of them could do. There was also an insidious effort to keep Moffat out of Denver and the line never did enjoy a favorable spot at Union Station. They were set apart at 15th and Delgany Streets so that passengers had to walk nearly a quarter of a mile. The old building erected by Moffat stands unattended, but with historical preservation status.

Although a tunnel under the mountains had originally been planned, its specific location and elevation were not actually settled until the early 1920s. This may have had an influence on investor financing. The uncertainty of the precise location of the tunnel before and after Moffat's death in 1911 and the limited investor funding from the beginning left no choice but to successfully complete a railroad line over Rollins Pass. The road had to be capable of year-round operation and the line was to extend into western and northwestern

Colorado to service the ranching, lumber, coal, and oil interests that had been known about for a long time. Once the operation was profitable and self-sustaining, the company leaders would turn to the matter of the 6.1-mile tunnel.

Of course, this bit of utopian thought was challenged daily by winter operating costs that erased any profitable freight or passenger revenue. It may come as a shock that 41 percent of the operating budget went for snow management. At or around timberline, there are basically two seasons—lingering winter and a relatively short summer—which can change in an afternoon. On the other hand, most men enjoyed working in the mountains. The alpine beauty and immense grandeur of the summer were a kind of compensation. Winter, of course, brought the risk of sickness and freezing from exposure—along with the danger of injury or death from the heavy equipment operating within close quarters.

Corona was actually well appointed in a rough way. The top of the pass is situated on a broad and relatively flat saddle. After 1905, two snow sheds, centered at the top, extended for about a mile. There were living quarters for the diner operator and his spouse and the dispatchers operating the telegraph and later the telephone. Crew facilities were located in boxcars that had been heavily winterized and either placed adjacent to the tracks or integrated into the snow shed as apartments. There was access into the living quarters directly from the snow shed and to the outside from the opposite door. There were also insulated boxcars positioned to hold food supplies and parts for repairs, etc. Boxcars in those days were smaller than present-day units; however, for the first two or three years, small log cabins pictured in old photographs were built alongside the tracks. Some may have remained in use until the operation ended.

A large water tower, heavily insulated with sawdust, stood near the center of the settlement. Water was pumped up by a steam pump from a small lake named Pump House Lake, situated a few hundred feet below and west of the top of the pass. A solitary individual manned the pumping operation on a year-round basis. The historical account is that, once a year, a supply of coal was delivered and was somehow slid down by wagon and pulley. A cable was strung between the top and his cabin to guide him and to hang on to when he visited Corona. The pay was reportedly fifty-eight cents an hour, but it was for a twenty-four-hour day and every day. Despite the isolation and risk of sickness or accident, the operator and those who followed might have accumulated some money.

Corona enjoyed steam heat from two boiler plants—thanks to the water supply from below—as well as electric lighting and telephone service, which did not replace the telegraph.

The diner was open around the clock. The diner served crews, passengers, and tourists. The nearby hotel was a stone building built on a spectacular spot in 1913. It boasted steam heat and electricity, but only stood for a few years before being torn down. The incessant wind and arctic chill made an otherwise stunning experience impractical. Food prices at the diner were high as might be expected, and the crews were issued subsidized company meal tickets with the cost deducted from their pay.

## Experiments

In 1904, locomotive engineer Sterling Way was challenged by Ridgeway to try to "buck up the hill" without a helper engine and open a snowbound track, since one of the only two snowplows they possessed was out of service. Ridgeway, who was formerly superintendent of construction, realized that he knew little about the technique and deferred to the locomotive engineer. Just about everything during those early times was trial and error—and certainly was so with snow management. Way accepted the challenge. He understood the necessity of the assignment and the limits of a steam engine. He could somehow calculate the depths of a snowdrift plunge ahead and retreat just in time to avoid the powerful engine stalling and dying. Way successfully worked up the west side through the snowdrifts from Arrow to Ptarmigan Point and the safety of a snow shed. The roadbed was still incomplete to the west beyond Arrow.

## Leaders

The leader and most liked and respected man in the field was Joe Culbertso, known as "J. B.," a native of Chariton, Iowa. He was the chief dispatcher and controlled the contingent of men and machines while coping with their daily problems. Culbertson, barely five feet tall, was working for the Burlington and Missouri Railroad as a telegrapher and dispatcher in 1903 as the Denver, Northwestern, and Pacific Railroad Company was just getting started. His superintendent, perhaps reflecting on his own progress, urged the young man to look west and get in on the ground floor with a new line going straight west out of Denver and over the mountains.

Railroad work on the mountain was dangerous for any employee. Conductors, switchmen, brakemen, and laborers were a dedicated lot. Much of the success of the line during the twenty-six years that Rollins Pass was under construction and operational can be attributed to them and their personal qualities. A special form of bonding grew out of the peculiar difficulty and dangers of the job. And, once on the mountain, there was no easy way to quit. Winds were generally constant and could be so fierce that rail cars would be blown off the tracks and men off of high trestles. One unknown worker described the experience as a blowing, freezing hell. Twenty-four-foot snowdrifts were not uncommon—along with scattered snow cover well into summer.

The Moffat line was barely operating in 1903 when the newspapers began following every scrap of information that passed their way. The Colorado Railroad Museum in Golden, Colorado, holds a manuscript section that reveals some glimpses of the period. On May 11, 1903, *The Denver Post* printed an article describing the ongoing contentious challenge by those against Moffat and suggesting that he would fail in his attempt to reach Salt Lake City.

E. H. Harriman, chief officer of the Union Pacific, was determined to leave no stone unturned in stopping David Moffat, including recruiting others to combat Moffat. An article in *The Denver Post* carried the story.

When United States Senator William A. Clark bought the Oregon Short Line property south of Salt Lake City he promised to make no connection with the Moffat line, according to current report. It is understood that Clark has joined with Harriman and as a result to build into Salt Lake City would only mean to battle the Moffat Line at that point. In other words, it could not participate in through Pacific coast business. This move is looked upon as a checkmate for the Moffat road, with the result that the Rio Grande will build to a connection and the Union Pacific will do the same, leaving the Moffat a purely local mountain road and subject to only such business as the Gould and Harriman roads propose to turn over to it, except what originates on the line.

Moffat took the high view and publicly discounted the attacks. He said, "I started out to build to Salt Lake, and only death or a shortage of money can stop me."

David Moffat maintained that he was unaware of any Eastern scheme to block his plans, but this is hardly convincing inasmuch as Harriman and Gould were resolute in their early blockage of his financing with Wall Street interests. In fairness to Harriman and the Union Pacific, the company was under an economic threat to complete certain sections of the road to qualify for government land grants. A tunnel diversion or even an earlier 104-mile spur from Cheyenne into Denver was out of the question. On a lighter side, the railroad's potential customers in western Colorado were anxious to use the line despite all the outside venom. The first shipment into Denver was recorded in *The Denver Post* on September 13, 1904. Three carloads of wheat were carried the prior day over Rollins Pass. It was the first year of regular operation, and the line had barely struggled over Rollins Pass three months earlier in June 1904.

> Wheat has begun to move over the Moffat road. It signalizes the opening of the railroad to freight. The first shipment was made yesterday, three cars of wheat having been brought from the farm of Thomas F. Tucker to Utah Junction and turned over to the Colorado and Southern for shipment to Golden where it will be milled. On the ranch of Mr. Tucker is 11,000 bushels of wheat and it will all be carried on the new railroad to this city.

The Moffat passenger terminal in the rail yards was a source of conflict for years. One of the weapons used on Moffat was to hamper his access, and passengers would have to walk a considerable distance. Moffat had earlier established an agreement with the Colorado and Eastern Railroad (a nearly defunct line) permitting the Moffat line to use the Colorado and Eastern right of way into downtown Denver. Reportedly, there was an outstanding option to buy the right of way, which would put pressure on the Moffat adversaries to release their interests in the twenty-one-mile right of way, which included the essential six-mile leg into Denver, which Moffat needed. *The Denver Post* carried an October 7, 1903 column suggesting that a terminal association was being considered to consolidate the rail lines around Denver and do away with the costly transfer and switching charges between different lines. A lawsuit was even filed by an investor who felt threatened by the plans. Reportedly there were plans for the Moffat road, Denver and Rio Grande, and the Rock Island to share the Colorado Eastern right of way into Denver. Strength in small numbers might help.

A July 31, 1904 article reported that Moffat—with some of his investors—had designed a strategy to redevelop the old Delgany Street terminal facility where they were operating. They planned to remake it over into a new Union Station, replacing the present building. The Moffat people had always resented the imposition that had been put on them by the stronger Harriman and Union Pacific forces, and this was the perfect counterpunch. Much of the redevelopment area was part of a fifteen-lot tract called River Front Park, which exists today. The anti-Moffat forces, after regrouping, were able to prevail over the redevelopment threat, but they were aware that the Moffat group could strike back. A very nice terminal building was built and used over the Moffat period. For many years, it has stood silent and neglected in the face of lower downtown redevelopment. Today, the structure is at least protected by historical designation status.

On March 9, 1906, *The Denver Post* speculated that Moffat was not really in charge of his line—Eastern interests instead were in control. Moffat denied the assertions as always, but they persisted nevertheless.

> It is believed in Denver that D. H. Moffat no longer has a controlling interest in the Moffat Road, but that it will be built through to Salt Lake City under his direct supervision, and will continue to bear his name. What interests are behind the road are concealing themselves for the present.

The Burlington line, a Gould holding, was a constant in-your-face irritant to Moffat operations. According to a January 1906 local news article, Burlington officials reportedly were preparing another challenge to the Moffat right of way far to the west in Routt County. The Denver, Utah, and Pacific Railway Company had been around since 1880 and held some right-of-way rights. Moffat had even been one of the original investors. The company—now controlled by Burlington—argued against the Moffat assertion that Moffat's legally purchased right-of-way rights were invalid. Colorado courts had held that rights-of-way are nontransferable. Moffat's attorneys were instead able to prevail based on the argument that the line had been abandoned before Burlington took possession.

Skirmishes continued nearly up to the time of the Moffat tunnel construction. Even some fishermen objected in what would be a common practice a century later. On July 21,1906 *The Denver Post* reported that railroad construction in Rock Creek Canyon, a few miles west of McCoy, had threatened to dam the creek flow.

For a while, David Moffat was able to finance his operation with his own resources along with the help of a relatively small group of backers. A March 9, 1906 news story reported that Moffat was releasing $10 million of his prior pledge of $20 million of authorized 4 percent gold bonds to go toward further financing. If the public had lacked confidence in Moffat, he would not have been able to hold on. At about the same time, the Department of Justice signaled that it would not reopen the Gore Canyon case. This was good news—and it assured Moffat and his people that the blasphemous distractions would not be repeated.

Moffat was reported at one point to have seriously considered abandoning the project because of the costs until Samuel Perry, one of his organizers, accompanied Colonel D. C. Dodge on a trip to his home in Steamboat Springs. Dodge, because of his age and circumstances, declined to invest in the line, but he did establish the Denver and Steamboat Construction Company, which did some work for the Moffat line under favorable terms. Dodge also helped raise funds to extend the line to Steamboat Springs.

## General Notice

To enter or remain in service is an assurance of willingness to obey the rules. Obedience to the rules is essential to the safety of passengers and employees, and to the protection of property. The service demands the faithful, intelligent, and courteous discharge of duty. The Company is dependent on the traveling and shipping public for its earnings. Therefore it is necessary that each employee use his best endeavors to serve this Company's patrons and the community at large, faithfully, intelligently, and courteously. To obtain promotion, capacity must be shown for greater responsibility. Each employee, in accepting employment, assumes its risks and is expected and required to look after and be responsible for his own safety, as well as to exercise care to avoid injury to others. In case of doubt, adopt the safe course. Speed must always be sacrificed to safety.

The Denver and Salt Lake Railroad Company
Train Rules
Operating Department
Effective October 1, 1913

# CHAPTER 6:
# THE ROLLINS PASS TRAIL AND JOHN QUINCY ADAMS ROLLINS

When David Moffat's engineers decided on the location of the railroad line, they were following the steps of timeless travelers. The Ute Indians in the region had always used the trail over the Continental Divide between the eastern slope and Middle Park in present-day Grand County. After Berthoud Pass was opened over the same mountain, the Indians still preferred their own route. The trail eventually carried the informal name of Boulder Pass. The headwaters of South Boulder Creek are within the crossing region, so the reference is logical. Prior to the Boulder Pass name, the trail was reportedly referred to by whites as the Hill, Hell's Hill, and probably any assortment of names. The Indians surely must have had their own name for the place. And the early-day mountain men carried with them their own manner of reference.

Although Middle Park was considered a Ute Indian reservation until 1878, white men did venture into the stunning isolation. Moreover, the Utes spent considerable energy resisting the Cheyenne and Arapaho annual hunting parties, and there is archeological evidence that the Ute's went so far as erecting stone fortifications.

In July 1865, William N. Byers, owner of *The Rocky Mountain News*, and his brother Frank, along with I. P. Van Wormer and a Negro employee, took two wagons over the trail to present-day Hot Sulphur Springs. Byers had acquired the springs a year earlier from the Ute Indians and he may have traveled there to inspect and improve the property or more likely enjoy the fascination of the region. His first trip had reportedly been by way of Berthoud Pass. The Indians visited the springs whenever they wished to, and Byers was careful never to interfere. There is the story that Ute Chief Ouray was brought to the springs in the fall of 1866 to treat his severe rheumatism. His party carried him there on a blanket tied between two poles and dragged along by an Indian pony—travois style. Ouray was known to have learned to read and write to a limited extent, and when he left, he scrawled with a piece of charcoal on the door of Byers cabin, "Hep good Ura." It was one of the occasional warm moments between the two cultures that remains eternal.

Two years earlier, during the fall of 1864, a government wagon train with twenty-two wagons traveling between Fort Douglas, Utah, and Fort Leavenworth, Kansas, passed through western Colorado and over the pass. This was no doubt an experimental route rather than the usual trek across Wyoming. History records that they followed Indian trails along Ranch Creek on the west side and Jenny Creek on the east. The logistics of the trip had to have been prohibitive, but then they did things like that during those days. A small contingent of soldiers were reportedly garrisoned in Middle Park as early as 1863 and they had to be periodically supplied. John Fremont was to have traveled the trail in 1844. Two of his men are supposedly buried on the east side. In 1865, John Rollins led a party of one hundred Mormons and thirty-nine wagons westward over the road. There are historical questions as to this or that wagon train, how many people were with the train, and the exact dates of passage. Probably there were more than officially counted, but most of those details are lost to time.

### John Quincy Adams Rollins

John Rollins was born in Germantown, New Hampshire, on June 16, 1816. His father was a Baptist minister. As a young man, John Rollins worked in Boston in a variety of jobs and later in real estate in Chicago. He also freighted lumber on the Mississippi River before moving West. In 1836, Rollins married Louisa Burnett. She died in 1880 at present-day Rollinsville, which her husband first founded as the town of South Boulder. They had one son, John III, but his records may be lost. He married Emma Chapin Clark in 1881 and she died in Denver in 1938 at age ninety-six.

## Making His Mark

After arriving in Denver on a wagon train in 1860, Rollins promptly headed for the mining camps, eventually settling along the upper reaches of South Boulder Creek (west of present-day Rollinsville and above present-day Nederland). The upper elevations are mostly open land. By all accounts, Rollins was a good citizen. On one occasion, he was reportedly paid a generous compliment by a local resident, Ovando Hollister, who, in a moment of total giving, reportedly depicted Rollins as the most energetic man in the world. In any event, Rollins was an active person. Some recollection might be noteworthy.

In 1860, soon after arriving in Colorado, Rollins helped found the town of Cherokee City at "the junction of the Cache la Poudre and South Platte Rivers." The name would later change to Latham and finally present-day Greeley and adjacent Evans, sixty-five miles north of Denver. As mentioned, he founded South Boulder, now Rollinsville, the last town on the east side of the Moffat Tunnel. During its heyday, the place had some ore-stamping mills, and there was a limited attempt to introduce farming into the immediate area where the elevation is some 8,500 feet above sea level. Rollinsville was also a stage stop along present-day Highway 119. The building is still used. Rollins and his Rollins Gold Company held some four hundred mining lode claims, which were an integral part of his wealth—many were acquired from payment of delinquent taxes during the 1860s.

Between 1864 and 1879, Rollins held contracts to improve the Boulder Pass Wagon Road, which can be accessed today at certain points using a Department of the Interior USGS Historic Trail map during the summer and fall. There was no letup, however, on getting across the mountains west of Denver. On February 10, 1865, the territorial legislature awarded a charter to the Overland Wagon Road Company to build a suitable road over Boulder Pass beginning in Denver, Boulder City, and Boulder Pass or nearby Arapahoe Pass—and without tollgates between Denver and Boulder City. Ben Holladay—the Stagecoach King, as he was known—and his cousin and attorney, General Bela M. Hughes, were the primary corporate organizers. Bela Hughes had presided over the final months of the bankrupt Central California Overland and Pikes Peak Express stage line, which Holladay would take possession of in November 1860.

The elevation quickly presented a rigorous 2,500-feet change from the valley floor to the top of the pass. Travelers on foot and horseback, wagons, and working livestock all suffered the strains of exhaustion to make a road to—and over—the top. On a later test run, Bela Hughes and his party left Salt Lake City on June 3, 1865, with 150 men and twenty-two wagons, crossing western Colorado and Boulder Pass. The trip reportedly took four months. On February 5, 1866, another charter was issued to the Overland Wagon Road Company to develop Berthoud pass. The final approaches to Berthoud Pass then and now can be regarded as steep and the working expedition apparently did not progress very well. The original road bears little or no reference to the present road for vehicles. There was a lot of disassembling wagons and pulling them up and down the trail. Today, part of the west side road is an isolated ski trail to the bottom. Glimpses remain on the east side as well.

The Colorado territorial legislature recognized Rollins's contributions to the region and, on February 6, 1866, established the Middle Park and South Boulder Wagon Road. It would be a toll road. John Rollins, Perley Dodge, and Frederic Weir held the ten-year franchise. The fee for a single team would be $2.50 and various charges for different teams and loose livestock. It isn't mentioned, but Native Americans' fees were normally waived on toll roads. The wagon road is usually in close proximity to the later Moffat railroad bed. Road construction was finally completed in 1873.[1]

John Rollins in his business expanse even formed a freighting partnership with David Butterfield who had established the David

Butterfield Dispatch stage line as well as his freight line. Butterfield (no relationship to John Butterfield) started the famed Smoky Hill freight wagon and stagecoach route. Ben Holladay took over the line in March 1866 after bankruptcy. Rollins reportedly lost $75,000 in the venture. As mentioned earlier, Rollins was a minerals investor and may have invested in a hotel at Cheyenne, Wyoming, in 1868. He was a principal organizer in 1880 of the Denver, Rollinsville, and Western Railroad, which did nothing and—not surprisingly—he was elected mayor of Rollinsville in 1881. The following year, the couple moved to Denver. John Rollins died on June 20, 1894, at age seventy-eight. He is buried at Riverside Cemetery, Denver's oldest cemetery.

## A Lighter Side

John Quincy Adams Rollins had a lifelong interest in billiards. It may be anecdotal, but sometime in 1866, probably in an off moment, he reportedly challenged a fellow player and they agreed on a $400-bet limit per game. The contest went on for a day and a half as each man's skill and luck ebbed and waned. Finally, Rollins, with a $12,000 winning position, called it quits and pocketed $11,000 after the $1,000 forfeiture fee they had agreed to.

His business exposure and the billiards avocation occasionally caught up with him and there is a lengthy list of newspaper accounts in the Western History section of the Denver Public Library. By all accounts, John Quincy Adams Rollins gave much to his adopted state.

## Pleasure and Danger

Forest Crossen's job at Corona left him with time to explore and hike around the area. One afternoon, his new friend Henry Jones invited Crossen to what could have been fatal hike after some sightseeing. Crossen said,

> We started back to Corona, decided to go up the railroad track. Beyond the tunnel we entered a half snow shed built into the side of a hill. It was a dark, forbidding-looking place,

black as the pit from the coal smoke of locomotives and rotary plows thundering through. The ice that had accumulated from the eight-month winter was frightening. Green, streaked with black, it looked abysmally old. At each side it rose in a thick wall, with only the scantiest clearance for the Mallet's big low pressure cylinders. In the short alpine summer, it was melting, but very slowly.

Suddenly Jones stopped and listened. Then he grabbed my wrist and ran for the portal of the shed. Once outside, we leaped to one side, hearts beating wildly. Presently we heard a faint *hiss, hiss, hiss* that grew louder. A Mallet locomotive, returning to Tolland light, eased slowly out of the shed. I don't think I have ever seen a locomotive move so slowly. The hiss was air compressed in the cylinders escaping. As the huge locomotive eased by, the big compound cylinders in front sticking far out at each side, I realized our close call. Had we been caught far in the shed, we could not have climbed those walls of ice. We would have been dead men. Even now, the memory of it makes me shudder.

## Denver Public Library, Western History Section, ca 1903-1927

*David Moffat*

*Tunnel Construction*

*Corona*

*Former hotel at Corona*

*Snow drifts*

*Rotary snow plow*

*Snow shed at Corona*

*East portal*

*Moffat terminal at Denver*

*Climbing Rollings Pass 4% grade*

*Snow shed at Corona*

**Arrow**

*Tolland Inn*

*Track laying machine*

*West portal*

*Tunnel near completion*

*Tressel and tunnel*

*Yankee Doodle Lake*

*Tunnel No. 3*

*Bull gulch*

*Picnickers arriving at Tolland*

*Excursion passengers*

*Rollingsville*

*Gore Canyon*

*Gore Canyon*

*Winter dining*

# CHAPTER 7:
## DANGEROUS TRIAL AND ERROR

A rotary plow had not been ordered at the outset of work on Rollins Pass, and the crews were into their second winter season. Moffat was holding costs down and gambling on a mild winter. It was a mistake. The gambling tables would have provided better odds. Maintenance of the line and the tunnel construction—or the chipping away at it because a final site had still not been settled—was swallowing up any semblance of a budget. All that the early crews had available to fight the snowdrifts were a couple of V-shaped plows. One was mounted on a flat car and weighted down with rocks and boulders.

The heavy paralyzing snows and fierce arctic weather were late in arriving in 1904, and the crews had kept the pass reasonably open, but a clicking of the telegraph signaled trouble on the west side. Snow was drifting heavily, and the extra engine—operated by engineer Frank Campbell and his crew—was responsible for keeping the snow flanged out before it would drift into an unmanageable condition. From some later personal interviews, probably in the 1940s, with Joe Culbertson, George Barnes, and others, Bollinger collected a story about one of the early challenges. Over the telegraph came this cryptic message: "The extra No. 179 East had not been heard from." Joe Culbertson intently listening to his telegraph key, and he deftly tapped back an answer.

Culbertson of course had the responsibility to coordinate train traffic for safe separation. The train coming up from the west had made the first six miles with little delay while cleaning out both ends of tunnel thirty-three on the west side where snow was drifting badly. Frank Campbell had driven his engine around the Loop and now was gaining some speed for a snow drift after he crossed the trestle. He managed to get through the drift, but a little further on, the grates for some unknown reason fell out of the firebox and down onto the ash pan. The engine of course had suddenly lost its fire, and prompt emergency procedures were called for. Culbertson had a major problem with a lost engine and Campbell's disabled engine, which was yet to be accounted for.

Campbell shut his steam off to conserve what remained, and he made a quick decision to briefly stop and back down into the relative safety of the Loop siding and try to secure the grates. Otherwise the engine would have to be drained—a very difficult job in severe weather. Campbell had no difficulty in coasting the locomotive down to Loop siding, where he dumped the coals onto the rail bed to lessen the heat and eliminate the smoke and gas. Engines were equipped with slash bars and clinker hooks to manage the fire, and as he worked to recover the grates, his fireman worked at the same task under the engine. In short, it was about like working inside and around a cramped, still-hot, and dangerous fireplace. In the freezing weather the engine cooled down sufficiently so that the two men working together could restore the grates. Since it was a cold night, the flues remained warm enough to form a natural suction to pull the coal gas up from under the engine into the firebox where Campbell was working. Unfortunately, danger can be a cruel companion, and within the confines of the firebox, he inhaled the lethal mixture into his lungs. It was a terrible experience, but the grates were finally replaced. The gunnysacks which he used for cushions and protection from the remaining heat, were now soaked with engine oil. Borrowing kindling from the caboose, Campbell and his fireman built a new fire in the engine. Two hours or more were lost during this chilling recovery, which permanently injured Frank Campbell's lungs. In his selfless effort, he was able to save an expensive engine and limit disruption to the line.[1]

Most of the Moffat people were like this. Frank Campbell's loyalty to his duty cost him his health—his lungs would no longer tolerate the Rollins Pass elevations. The company transferred him to a lower altitude as a hostler at the Utah Junction outside of Denver operating yard engines, but he eventually had to give this up. The benefit of workmen's compensation was something in the future.

## Carrying the Mail

Racing ahead of a storm or successfully struggling through one presents an opportunity for those who like to tell stories and exchange events with eager listeners of some earlier drama they might have experienced or heard about. Berthoud Pass skirts the southern part of James Peak. The railroad crossed over the northern flanks of the same peak. The pass is now US 40. This is a story about a crossing related by a train passenger, now lost to history, to his fellow travelers as they waited during an engine stop to take on water while on their way over Rollins Pass.

The story begins at Cottonwood Pass. It may have even been a yarn. It is significant to remember that moving the mail around the West was always considered a priority. Sometimes it was carried by contract carriers and at other times by private service. The early stage lines set the standard, and railroads and individuals bore their share. Cottonwood Pass lies west between Tabernash and Granby. It originally served as a shortcut to the Grand County seat at Hot Sulphur Springs. Today it is an easy drive in good weather—scenic and still somewhat isolated.

The exact date is not known. It could have been anytime between 1903 and 1910. Four locomotives in tandem each took on water as usual at Jenny Lake. In the meantime, the storyteller began the story as a storm raced across the tops of the peaks just 1,500 feet above the small group. Violent drafts of arctic wind would race down on the train, sweeping away bits of warmth from the steam-heated passenger cars. The wind even seemed to join in the story, which was said to have occurred around 1892. It seems a man carrying the mail on foot stopped at the Button Ranch on Cottonwood Pass. His destination was Empire and then Georgetown on the east side of Berthoud Pass—not an easy trip. Button, the rancher, for unknown reasons, decided to travel along with the carrier, and he even bundled up his granddaughter, Daisy, who was about age seven. Georgetown enjoyed more amenities than Middle Park could offer, so the trip was perhaps understandable. The passenger continued the story. It might have been from his own experience or from someone close to him or again even a yarn. It seems the point of the story was the mail must get through, but sometimes it did not.

> We got on the cutter [a light sleigh] and drove up through Fraser and past Cozen's Ranch [now an historical point]. It was getting so dark by the time we got to the Old Fritz Ranch at Vasquez [present-day Hideaway Park], we decided to stay overnight. When we went into the ranch cabin, the snow was so deep it was like going down into a cellar to get into the house. Our beds were crudely built bunks on the side of the room.

> Next morning, we got on the cutter and started for the pass, two or three miles distant. At first the two horses had no trouble pulling us two men and Daisy, but when we got near the top, the storm was so bad we put on our snowshoes and broke trail for the horses leaving the mail on the sled and little Daisy to drive the team. In fact, the blizzard was so terrible on the top we finally covered her up with a blanket and continued breaking trail for the team on the way up. We had not gone far on the east side until the weather was different. In fact, we left our sled and borrowed a wagon, which we used for the rest of the trip.

The storyteller, now lost to history, continued reminiscing how the mail did not always get through—and neither did the train. Those who were foolhardy often paid with their lives. "They did not want to be found 'frost-killed,' as we used to call it. In the spring, sometimes we would find men frozen to death sittin' on tree stumps."

The chilling story ended as the four engines were finally watered, and the trip to the top was renewed. Unknown to the souls on the train, the first of many blockades of the line lay just ahead, and they would have their own story to tell future listeners or relate again the prior story.

As the lead engine steamed over where the Rollins Pass and Rollins Wagon Road intersected, crusted ice that had built up to the top of the track derailed the locomotive. A messenger was sent up the tracks to Corona to summon help, returning with twenty-five men who had been working on snow shed construction. They would try to re-rail the engine. It would be the first of many incidents. Derailment would happen many times until the hydraulic-operated ice chisels were placed under most of the engines to clear the rails.

Under the driving wind and subzero wind chill, the shivering workers could do nothing. The three pusher engines and their cars disconnected and backed down the hill a short distance while the crew blocked the wheels. The passengers and crew scrambled to the safety of the partially built Corona snow shed. Bob Bishop, the engineer, and the fireman, George Clarke, were last to shut down their engine to bank some critical heat for later resumption. Re-firing a dead engine would be a monumental task and would tie up the line even more. Both men hovered close to the rapidly cooling firebox to get warm before moving to the top and safety. Along the way to safety, the engineer and fireman stumbled upon a disoriented, nearly frozen bridge carpenter sitting on a boulder. The two somehow carried him in to a secure area, although he later lost some fingers. The prior mail carrier story, probably an anecdote, may have carried some truth and a warning.

The Main Range Tunnel (Moffat Tunnel as it was known) was projected to take three years to build, and the pass would be abandoned. Instead, Rollins Pass would remain operational from 1904 until Sunday, February 28, 1928, when the first official train with dignitaries passed through the tunnel, meeting an unhappy group at the west portal. They were unhappy because they had thoughtlessly been overlooked from participating by *The Denver Post*, which sponsored the inaugural event. Most of the population in the Fraser Valley was there, and with the direction of Dr. Susie Anderson, they angrily prepared a large sign for the dignitaries to see as they emerged from the tunnel: WE BUILT THE TUNNEL, THE POST DIDN'T.

The rails over the pass remained until pulled up in 1935. The old route was reportedly used on occasion. A desperately needed rotary plow that the line could call its own was finally delivered and placed in use on February 10, 1905. It cost $22,476, which was a lot of money at the time, and immediately broke down after stripping its blades while moving through a snow slide that included rocks and snapped trees. The machine was quickly rebuilt at the Denver shops with tougher steel blades and put back into service—and the crews were more careful. The author has been around old rotary snow plows, and it is a monumental task to work on one.

**Stalled on the Pass**

The ever-present threat of being stalled on the pass during a raging storm was a constant worry. A few hours of intense snow and wind would alter everything. Even in summer weather, a breakdown brought difficulties. Mountain lightning, especially in the early to midsummer, was a threat. Stoppages rippled through the chain of authority from brakeman to engineer to conductor and all along the line to the superintendent down in Denver—even David Moffat probably would have known something about it.

The line would be crippled by a lack of facilities on the top half, mainly water storage, until the summer of 1905. After a hard pull upward from Jenny Lake, the water levels in the tenders would usually be too low to continue down the west side, and the engines would have to back down to re-water and proceed up again while smashing through newly drifted snow. With the lives of men and their equipment on the line, there was little room for error or bad judgment. The Moffat people would eventually manage situations that few railroaders would ever face. The logistics were time consuming, repetitive, and costly. If it had not been for the integrity and determination of the crews during those experimental years from 1903–1906 or later, the project might have failed.

As mentioned, the water problem on top at Corona had to be dealt with and quickly. There were two lakes in the nearby area. One is barely accessible, several hundred feet immediately below Corona. The second is reasonably close—west and slightly down from Corona—and was assigned the name Pump House Lake. By summer 1905, water was being drawn and pumped up to supply the Corona facilities. During the winter, lake water was probably first warmed by a boiler at the lake and then pumped up to Corona where it was again reheated for steam heat.

Arrow, on a bluff above the Fraser Valley on the west side of the pass, was usually a safe haven for trains and crews if they could get there. Nevertheless, February 10, 1905, promised to be another unforgiving day. Bollinger deftly relates the challenge of leadership.

The rotary plow, pushed along by two engines pulling two cars full of food and supplies along with a tool car and two cabooses, left Tolland early in the morning headed west. The snowplow pilot operating the rotary was Billy Woodruff. Mike Broderick was the conductor. Fuller and Sterling Way were the locomotive engineers. Also riding with them were trainmaster Edgar and special conductor George Barnes.

The employee classification was simply what took place at the time; a trainmaster was responsible for all of the trains on his line after they were released by the yardmaster. The yardmaster, of course, had control of trains within the rail yard. A conductor was the chief authority of his train, and he answered to the trainmaster. The engineer, fireman, brakeman, etc., fell into a generally descending order. Dispatchers and station operators were more on the order of a liaison between the chains of authority. The position of roadmaster referred to someone who had the responsibility of track conditions and safety measures. The job titles and functions have changed little over the years, aside from modernization. Bollinger narrates.

Drifting snow could build up so quickly that coupling two trains with as many as four locomotives was a common technique. The arctic-like winds would reposition drifts that often would form into huge frozen seas of snow. At other locations the vagaries of the wind would keep the tracks clear. February 10 promised to be a long day for this crew.

At Jenny Lake, the tracks were typically blown free of snow, and the engine tenders were filled with water, brakes tested, and a couple of long whistles signaled readiness as the lonely group departed upward in the cold chill. The train quickly met the first of a series of drifts as the rotary chewed forward, the water levels supplying the steam for the rotary and the pusher engines were rapidly depleted. The nearest water was at Sunnyside on the west side, two-and-a-half miles down from the top. Pump House Lake, as mentioned, would be finished that summer in 1905—an eternity in that harsh environment.

Late in the day, the engines and their crews finally reached the relative safety of the uncompleted Corona snow sheds, and there was total agreement among the crew that any further progress was out of the question. There was not enough water to provide the steam to operate the air brakes over any descending distance.

However, Edgar, the trainmaster, overruled conductor George Barnes and ordered the men to shovel snow into the tender. He reasoned the engine heat would gradually turn the snow to water. It took a lot of powdery snow to do much, but it was the only choice under the circumstances. The procedure was used frequently later on, but in a wild wind, the shoveled snow carrying little moisture disappeared into the air rather than the tender. At 11,000 feet, those workers—even in the best of conditions—tired rapidly. Finally, after lots of shoveling, there was enough water in the tender that was estimated to make it down to safety. The rotary plow leading the small train cautiously crept out of the snow shed, cutting through the ten-to-twelve-foot drifts, and slowly led the group down the hill toward Arrow and warmth and safety.

The brakemen probably had the toughest job. They rode on top of the cars and were ready to twist down the brakes on each car if the brake lines froze or failed in any manner. The dangerous wind chill stabbed at them through their frosted clothing and made for a very dangerous job. Standing and walking on the roofs of moving and rocking rail cars was always risky and even more so with slippery conditions, limited visibility, and sudden gusts of wind. The slow ten- or fifteen-mile-per-hour speed over the road was a redeeming element.

At Ptarmigan Point, the engines stalled again from lack of water. Again the crew frantically shoveled snow, and the wind whipped the snow off the shovels. Marooned again one-and-one-half miles down from the top and one mile from Sunnyside and water, they were almost to the point where with sufficient steam for the brakes they could have coasted past Sunnyside and into Arrow, but it was not to be. In a frantic life-saving decision, the seven terrified passengers and a crewman appointed to be the leader were ordered to "hit the cinders—walk while there was still a chance!" One must experience the intensity of an alpine snowstorm to appreciate the situation facing the crew and passengers.

In the meantime, Trainmaster Edgar decided to walk back up the tracks to Corona (an even riskier decision) and have the station operator send an emergency message to the Tolland Station on the east to send two light engines to pull the stalled train back up into the Corona shed. George Barnes, who had been overruled earlier by Edgar about remaining at Corona and now ignored by Edgar, climbed a telegraph pole alongside the stalled train, which in this case meant standing on top of the snow and connecting his telegraph-sending unit to send an emergency message to Tolland. In two or three years, the telephone would join the telegraph. This kind of railroading was new and fast paced. It would be some time before the various emergencies would have some procedures attached to them.

Barnes's message was swift and to the point—and word of it soon got out to the public and became the material for news stories. The message said, "Engines gone dead because of low water and inability to shovel snow in the terrible gale."

The cold of the mountain night arrived, reminding the frightened crew of their situation. At high altitudes and little or no cloud cover, temperature drop can be swift. Barnes, now in charge, knew that the few sandwiches left over from lunch would not be enough for the crew. Looking over the waybills of lading, he noticed that the supply car contained food for Bill Wood's Commissary at Arrowhead, which provided food for the railroad crews and the loggers. The waybill identified now-frozen canned goods, potatoes, and several quarters of beef. An ax, which was part of the inventory, served as a knife for the beef, while Barnes carefully inventoried what was taken. The potbellied stoves in the two cabooses provided heat for warmth and cooking, while the crewmen were packed together for warmth. Card games, talking, griping, sharing the duty of carrying coal from the engine tender, and a slight chance of sleeping completed the long winter night. Every man knew in his own mind that the situation could get worse, even fatal. Over seventy direct miles away in Denver, David Moffat maintained a silent vigil.

Morning arrived with the news that the two rescue engines had reached the top of Rollins Pass at Corona, but they were also stalled for the usual lack of water. The four-mile, 4 percent grade up from Jenny Lake had taken its toll. Barnes sent a second message to Denver that he and his men were safe. In the meantime, the two cabooses were packed with men doing little or nothing. Barnes decided with his usual resolve that several of them, including himself, would volunteer to walk out to a better location where he could organize a competent relief effort for the remaining crew.

After designating some authority during his absence, there was the tiring walk back up the track through the drifted snow to Corona to dry and warm up and then the four-mile-or-so cold hike down the track to Jenny Lake 1,500 feet below and, from there, the relatively unobstructed leg down to Tolland.

Men sometimes do strange and impulsive things when they are under stress. The engineer, Sterling Way, reportedly seized a snow shovel and turned it into a sled. In a brief and dangerous slide, he descended the 1,500 feet to Jenny Lake, but there he would have a chilly and lonely wait until the others arrived. Of the nine volunteers, one chose to remain at the Antelope Station, while the other eight hiked several miles down to the base of the pass at Tolland. Six men decided to remain and enjoy the warmth and comfort of Tolland and the final two—Barnes and Way—elected to continue about five miles farther to Rollinsville, a railroad stop and stagecoach station. On their way down, a train coming up from Denver to Tolland picked them up.

After a turnaround and warm-up, they presumably were on their way home again. Denver greeted them with an often-typical spring-like day, although only a few hours earlier their lives had been at risk.

Denver and the adjacent Front Range, which extends from a one-mile elevation to over 14,000 feet (13,660 feet in this case) can present an array of mild, spring-like to arctic conditions, all within sixty miles.

The two would not get home that easily. Their return engine had other orders. At Leyden, the engine crew was to hook onto a load of coal and return to Tolland. Barnes had no intention of a repeat ride and notified Denver headquarters once again in detail about the dangerous situation on the pass. Now, instead of a train ride back to Tolland, he and Way rode the interurban streetcar from Leyden into Denver. In those days, streetcars ran all over the metropolitan and suburban areas and to some rural locations.

Meanwhile, management having been alerted by Barnes's distress messages, busily rounded up a rotary plow from the Colorado Midland Railroad, but the Moffat people still had much to learn about arctic weather. The snow was so deep and crusted that, until the drifts were dynamited to fall back onto the track, the rotary could do little. The sides of the rotary cut were hard as ice, and the rotary simply rasped against the drifts. Progress was in feet and yards.

The rescue team finally reached Corona at 3:00 p.m. on February 23, 1905, as the afternoon ushered in the colder night. It will never be known now, a century later, how many times the engines had to drive up the road and back down for water at Jenny Lake, only to repeat the process within the howling wilderness. As night fell, there must have been a sense of foreboding among the rescue crew.

The story ends with no injuries or fatalities, but the storm left its mark. The engines, cars, and cabooses were frozen to the tracks, and their journals or wheel bearings were frozen. After a lot of jerking and dragging by the recovery engines, the entire train was safely under the snow shed. The weather was just as cold, but they were at least out of the wind and in a safer environment.

## Riding in a Rotary

Powerful steam rotary plows—and Moffat had some of the largest—could barely cut through some of the drifts, but only after work crews had cleared the snow down to the height of the twelve-foot cutting wheel. A narrow, frozen slit was left to barely accommodate the engine and cars. There was no additional room when an engine passed through. To this was added a constant numbing subzero wind chill for those working outside. The line eventually owned three rotary plows and, on several occasions, would lease a smaller one from the Colorado Midland people. At least one plow was eventually stationed at Corona on continuous standby. During the later years, several snow plows regularly patrolled the pass on both sides.

Joe Culbertson reportedly rode in a rotary snowplow and remarked, "The plow created a lot of vibration and noise, but it was otherwise a warm environment." The plow, as one might expect, encountered trees, rocks, ice, and early on lost many rotary blades before it was replaced by heavier blades and skilled crew operators. A coded series of locomotive whistles controlled the operations. The plowing procedure that had been developed was to run an engine with two freight cars from Tolland up to Jenny Lake to connect with two engines pushing a rotary. An extra caboose was often added to carry men to shovel snow if necessary. Some of the labor crew was classified as skilled workers in the event that the engines broke down. This caution contributed to the 41 percent winter operating costs.

Communications on the mountain were by telegraph; later the telephone was used as well. The instruments were a lifeline to the outside—to Tolland on the east and Arrow on the west. The lines were usually busy with cryptic messages about snow cuts filling back in after being cleared, delayed and stalled trains, breakdowns, accidents, and the like—probably even some gossip, although the Denver office had a repeater that picked up everything.

The risk of derailment was a constant threat, and a miserable amount of work was involved in re-railing a heavy engine or plow, so the snowplow operator and the engineers in the pushing engines had to very carefully coordinate their work. The powerful Mallet locomotives (known as Mallets) could easily overcontrol the rotary plow ahead of them. This was before the time of fully constructed steel cars, and the units were always susceptible to the failure of their coupling braces or even the crushing of the car. The ultimate risk was going over the side into a 400–700-foot chasm. The operation required a surgical coordination of whistles and timing between the locomotive engineers and the rotary plow operator.

The pull up the eastern side of the pass always left the water level in the tender low, and the crews stopped at Jenny Lake to take on water before proceeding with the remaining four miles to the top. Water was gravity fed for a hundred yards or so to an insulated holding tank. During winter plowing, the snow pilot operating the rotary plow would periodically call for more steam, while the two engineers pushing the unit would tensely manage their throttles and brakes to avoid burying and stalling the rotary and a possible derailment. The trio would communicate with each other by engine whistles as they carefully pushed further upward through the cuts, which once again were usually filled by blowing snow.

As they cautiously crossed the naked trestles, the wind might be swirling the snow into an angry whiteout, buffeting the train. Finally, the security of the Corona snow shed would be reached where acrid smoke and gas from idling and departing engines greeted them, but at least they were under cover—even though the ventilation problem was a matter that was never resolved. Electric exhaust fans may have been considered, but that seems to be about as far it went.

However, the trip was not finished at Corona, and the crew soon had to work their way down the other side. Wind and weather patterns were different on each side of the pass, and different skills were required to manage the route. Drifting on the west side was more wind-driven, and drifts would reportedly extend a half-mile into the snow shed. After one full year of regular operations and several years wiser, Joe Culbertson realized that he was onto something very big.

# CHAPTER 8:
## IT IS NEVER ROUTINE

A n army of men was required to manage the logistics of a railroad, especially this particular road. There never seemed to be dull moments, but the on-the-ground supervisors and crews handily dealt with each problem. The mechanical interruptions from weather and breakdowns remained constant over the years. However, during the early period, this was the most demanding because each incident brought something new to understand and manage and an opportunity to establish procedures.

**Fire in the Tunnels**

Tunnel fires were an unexpected phenomenon and downright frightening. An out-of-control tunnel fire could destroy the wooden supports and cause an eventual collapse. Line blockage would then be a disaster. Fires could start in many ways: sparks or hot coals from a passing engine, a road crew trying to keep warm with an unattended fire, etc. And as the air currents moved up the canyon, the turpentine—now creosote—used to treat the wooden ties made an especially volatile mix.[1] Tunnel fires were a menace.

**Derailments**

Derailments were a major headache. The engines were heavy (about 104 tons) even by the standards of an earlier period, and all kinds of techniques were tried and tested to get an engine and other cars back onto the tracks. Most of the engines had smaller lead wheels located under the very front of the engine. They were referred to as the pony truck and were susceptible to jumping off the track. This was usually because of an ice buildup to the extent that the wheel(s) would not ride solidly on the rail, but instead would ride up on the ice and roll off the track. Also, strong lateral winds blowing against a boxcar—even today—can tip a car or blow it off the tracks. Moreover, rails out of alignment from extreme cold or heat can do their bit of mischief. It was up to an alert engineer and his crew to know when a derailment occurred and to stop the train as quickly and gently as possible. If the accident happened while on a grade of any consequence, blocking and braking were the first priorities. The recovery work usually fell to the gandy dancers—the laborers or section men on the line.

On March 21, 1905, while Denver was enjoying spring and a high of sixty-two degrees, at Rollins Pass the temperature had reached only thirty-two degrees by midday. April storms in the mountains brought more snow. What would be a blessing a hundred years later—a blessing for a state that had outgrown its water supply—was in 1905 just another problem to deal with.

April 11 brought with it a fire in Tunnel 20. The fire roared out of control until it burned itself out. That fire would be the first of many. The tunnel was blocked and the passengers were directed to walk outside around the tunnel and board an open flatcar that had backed down to the site to pick them up along with the mail and baggage. They were given a chilly ride to Tolland and some warm overnight quarters. At seven o'clock the following morning, the train—led by a snowplow—started up the pass, finally reaching Corona at 4:15 p.m.

## Derailed

After dinner, an attempt was made to move down, but the storm prevailed, and the train remained overnight. The next morning, the pony truck under the engine derailed, and section men were sent to dig out the ice and snow from the track. As noted earlier, the rotary cuts were the width of a locomotive. A sheer, icy wall provided mere inches between the engine and the snow bank. Many tragic accidents occurred within these tight quarters as well as within the dimly lit snow sheds with gas fumes and smoke swirling everywhere.

There was little progress with the re-railing attempt. While the storm howled around the gandy dancers, the men worked in the narrow slit first made by the rotary, and carved out a larger opening around the front of the engine and derailed pony truck. Physical exertion at high altitudes can be exhausting, and a sort of slow motion set in as, in this case, the lead workers attempted to fit a pair of two-foot-long wooden blocks adjacent to each rail. One block was placed on the inside of the rail, which required someone to squirm along between the tracks under the steaming locomotive, and another worker secured a block on the outside of the rail. The procedure had to be completed on both rails, and then the outer blocks were spiked with a steel "frog" to guide the wheels during the transition from the wooden blocks to the steel rail. The procedure normally worked, but not without some misses.

The first day ended with no real success, and as the second day was closing, lanterns were lit. There was some optimism that success might be at hand. Everyone was moved away to safety, and the lead engine, which was off the tracks, and the pusher engine (called a hogger) whistled three shrill calls in the chilling afternoon and gently pushed forward as their throttles were cracked. The powerful drive wheels spun, and sand was quickly applied, but the pony truck would not climb on the rails and tore loose the spiked-in frogs.

All the men were cold, tired, and bitter; some of the men were wet. A mood of disappointment set in, but they labored on in the cold and growing darkness until they could no longer manage the weather and exhaustion. Finally, the group stumbled back up to the Corona facilities. It would be April 29—eighteen days—before a small rotary plow, leased again from the Colorado Midland Railway, chewed its way up the pass only to stall at a drift, pull back, and then grind through freshly dynamited snow. On May 2—some six weeks later—the stalled Moffat rotary and the re-railed engine and cars were each pulled loose and dragged back up to the Corona snow shed.

Two days later, the train finally reached Arrow on the west side above the Fraser Valley. The story would repeat itself many times.

The citizens of Denver followed all of this and, for those who watched and listened, which included most people, it became obvious that any meaningful work on the tunnel was going to be postponed until the Rollins Pass operation was up and running. Two simultaneous feats were impossible.

As the tracks advanced down into the Fraser Valley, survey work was taking place in Gore Canyon about forty-five miles west just beyond Kremmling. Gore Canyon would prove to be a major engineering and legal challenge before the rails ever reached the canyon.

Western Colorado remained a remote region, but transportation between the scattered Moffat work units was necessary—and so were passenger connections at the advancing railhead. Stagecoaches met their riders at towns and makeshift railheads and carried them and some freight on to their remote destinations just as they had done so for over fifty years around the West. The stage lines would remain a mode of Western transportation until around 1920 in the remote areas. The Whipple and Shaw stage line, dating back to 1888, served local needs. During the early years, McCoy had a hotel, which accommodated Moffat travelers going on to Steamboat and Craig and into northeastern Utah. Like most stage lines, livestock was a big part of the operation—in this case, over a hundred horses.

The handful of automobiles that ventured over the rough roads—with their thin tires rupturing on the sharp rocks—did not dispel the sense of remoteness during a breakdown, nor were they capable of carrying much more than their occupants and some gear.

For railroad use, automobiles were first fitted with small railroad wheels to propel and guide the vehicle. Later, the rubber tires propelled the car along the tracks, and the railroad wheels merely guided the car. The latter method was little different than what is seen today.

Not many people today know about the Corona Hotel that stood on the very top of Rollins Pass during the earlier years. As mentioned, it was constructed in 1913 and was operational for only a few years. Some of the foundation stones remain today. Moffat revenue was still thin, and any tourist income beyond Tolland and its tourist facilities for Denver travelers was helpful. The view was spectacular, of course, but the facility was impractical in the best of seasons and could only be used for three or four months out of the year.

The crews and through passengers were housed in facilities that were an extension of the snow shed. The small diner had an entrance designed in a manner to keep out the locomotive smoke and gasses—or else the place would have been uninhabitable. Room accommodations were essentially boxcars, which were smaller in those days and were modified into insulated sleeping apartments.

There was still a bit of the Wild West at the time, and the Corona station suffered its one and only armed robbery of passengers and crewmen. The robbers took a modest amount of money along with the pocket watches that most men carried. No one was hurt, and the robbers were presumed to have escaped on horseback over nearby Rollins Pass Wagon Road or through the back country rather than using the rail bed. Besides, by then the telegraph line was buzzing.

By May 15, 1908, the tracks reached McCoy, which had an outbreak of smallpox. A quarantine of sorts was established and the passengers were unloaded a mile beyond the station where they caught the stage to Steamboat Springs.

# CHAPTER 9:
## GORE CANYON

It must have seemed to Moffat and his investors that every known business interest rallied against the Moffat people to prevent them from obtaining a right of way that was essential if the railroad was to go anywhere. Gore Canyon, just west of Kremmling and through which the Colorado River flows, was the obvious location for an efficient and direct path for the continuation of the line. The other rail lines must have thought so too because this was the spot where they focused their attempts to halt the operation.

Gore Canyon is a deep fracture in the earth with steep, generally unstable walls. The early surveyors had a difficult time making any headway, but it was the most direct and practical route for the railroad to follow the river. Today, it is part of a major transcontinental route.

Moffat had friends near and far and one of them, E. U. Spring of Kremmling, sent him a letter on February 2, 1903, while Moffat was in New York City, advising him that the Hydro-Electric Power Plant Company out of Denver and the New Century Power Company (from where wasn't mentioned) had filed to build a reservoir in the canyon that spring. The New Century was reportedly planning to purchase or control the Denver hydroelectric business. The threat impacted the other railroad lines since all of them—the Denver, Utah, and Pacific, Colorado Railways, Denver Rio Grande, Union Pacific, and

Western Colorado Railroad—had all filed on the canyon at one time or another.

Orchestrating much of this was E. H. Harriman and his Union Pacific interests. He allegedly induced individuals to file a blizzard of mining claims throughout Gore Canyon, and he created enough pressure on Wall Street so that no one would have anything to do with Moffat.[1]

Moffat responded by assembling a survey party to enter Gore Canyon and begin some renewed work on an old Burlington grade that had been surveyed several years earlier. A camp was established, and some token construction was apparently commenced. A reservoir would have been a big mistake. Besides wiping out the right of way, a reservoir would have flooded much of Middle Park. And the intrigue would not end. Byers Canyon—immediately west of Hot Sulphur Springs and several miles east of Gore Canyon—was reportedly part of a behind-the-scenes failed attempt to stop Moffat by damming up Byers Canyon.

An intense legal battle quickly erupted over the Gore project and was accompanied by renewed surveys and soil and geological testing. The outcome was that with excellent legal counsel, investors who wouldn't back down, and unexpected, but vital support from President Theodore Roosevelt, the Moffat position was able to prevail. Roosevelt, aware of the controversy, arranged to visit the site during one of his Western hunting trips.

The rock formations comprising the canyon would not support the immense pressures of a dam. Moreover, the broad flats at the immediate east entrance of the canyon were—and still are—excellent as hay meadows, but soil tests found the area to be mud flats. The Bureau of Reclamation officials, under intense interrogation by Moffat counsel, admitted to never preparing any cost estimates for the proposed project they had been coerced into by the power companies, and they agreed that Colorado would not benefit from such a project.

An angry Moffat lawyer arguing the case in Washington, DC secured an admission that the "Reclamation Dam" from a survey error was to be located on the top of a mountain, a mile distant. It was also determined that much of the presentations made in court by the opposition were simply dishonest. By the latter part of 1904, the Moffat efforts to resist the other lines and the power companies were successful. The right of way would be built and, in time, all of the surviving railroads would benefit. Boulder Dam in Nevada would later become the alternative to Gore Reservoir.

Harriman was well aware of Moffat's legal victory at Gore Canyon and Moffat's newfound support from President Theodore Roosevelt. At an earlier time, Harriman had enjoyed a favorable relationship with Roosevelt, and it must have felt more like a stinging rebuke. Sometime in 1904 or 1905, shortly after the legal episode, Harriman extended an invitation to Moffat to come to New York. He offered to buy Moffat out at 51 percent of his accrued investment in his railroad—and he seasoned the offer with some additional common stock. Harriman, in turn, pledged to complete the line to Salt Lake City. Moffat was furious, declined the offer, and returned to Denver convinced that he was pretty much on his own. Moffat was determined to oversee the completion of construction through Gore Canyon by 1907.[2]

# CHAPTER 10:
# DAY BY DAY

M offat and his investors had hoped for an early stream of revenue after the line reached over into Middle Park and certainly from the extensive coal fields farther west. Actually, the revenue from hauling coal was substantial, followed by lumber, livestock, some passengers, and mail. But out-of-control costs depleted any revenue. Typical incidents included an expensive locomotive tumbling several hundred feet into a canyon, injured crewmen, some deaths, delayed schedules, angry customers, and the expense of bitter winters with twenty-to-thirty-foot drifts. There was more than one infuriated rancher who was stuck on the mountain while his family had to manage the ranch—or even worse, the anxiety when a wife and children were temporarily marooned somewhere on the pass.

Another hazard was the shipping of livestock during the fall. With an early storm, they could easily die from exposure. In fairness, the railroad managed the risks rather well; however, these hazards left the Moffat pockets empty. Now with the tracks reaching only to Granby—twelve miles or so beyond Tabernash and eventually to Hot Sulphur Springs, Parshall, and Kremmling—the economic prospects were gloomy. Kremmling celebrated July 4, 1906, with the arrival of the train, but Kremmling could offer little of economic value. There was hardly anyone in the town or area. Today, it is a vibrant ranching and recreational region.

Tourist revenue was an early source of reliable income, and it came from the residents of Denver eager to leave the city for the mountains. Automobiles were barely around, and the notion of getting away and traveling into the nearby mountains through lots of tunnels was a drawing card. By 1904, a special train left Denver early each weekend morning for Mammoth or Tolland where tourist facilities had been built. There is still some evidence of the location. Individuals, couples, and families could enjoy a day or a weekend.

As part of a public relations effort, the marketing department had playing cards printed with mountain scenes, calendars, a descriptive pamphlet or two, and a host of other tourist attractions. Some fragile evidence of a long-ago era remains within the railroad museum's manuscript section.

For the more adventuresome, the railroad continued up to the visual splendor of Corona at a dizzying 11,660 feet where the hotel served meals in the summer. The railroad continued the excursion line for several years until automobiles and reliable roads became more commonplace. A popular weekend line carrying skiers and summer sightseers from Denver has replaced the long-ago excursion trains. Arrow is gone, but the immediate bluff below Arrow and above the Fraser Valley is filled with apartments, condos, and second homes for those who come to Colorado to ski and visit.

## Make-Do Repairs

It wasn't all that often, due to the size of the machinery, but on-the-road repairs occasionally were made so that the train would not be shut down until help arrived. The iron railroad wheel, at the time, had an outside iron tire that was heated and shrunk on the wheel in a manner similar to a wagon or stagecoach wheel. Sterling Way, the engineer, noticed that the tire was becoming loose on one of his drive wheels. If it fell off, the potential for serious damage to the engine—and even the crew—was very real. Way reportedly stopped at the Kremmling station and found some stove pipe material.

"With his fireman helping, Way wedged the drive wheel up slightly, so they could slip strips of stove pipe material between the outer tire and inner wheel." Still, more creativity was needed. "After the tire was first heated by engine oil and waste rags distributed entirely around the circumference of the tire, then the tire was allowed to cool and shrink tight on the wheel." Bollinger confirms that the train safely returned to the shops at Tabernash and passed inspection.[1]

Author's note: How heat of any significance could be developed and safely applied is a mystery.

# CHAPTER 11:
## NEAR DISASTER

A t its completion, the snow shed at Corona was over a mile in length, but it was still not enough. The shed had been built to accommodate multiple tracks. There were other shorter snow sheds at critical spots along the road. The western side, because of the prevailing winds, would fill with drifts at its entrance, extending inward for a half mile. The engines carved out a slit in the snow, which was usually packed seven feet above the track, leaving just enough room for the rotary plow, the locomotives, and the cars to squeeze through. There was no clearance for a man. The east side did not experience nearly as much snow and ice buildup. Coordinating train traffic was a difficult skill to learn; they used written train orders furnished to departing crews and telegraphed ahead to division points. A reliable pocket watch was essential. Even today, with wired rails, modern electronics, and written train orders, a close touch is still required.

Bollinger, in a later direct interview with conductor George Barnes, recounted a dramatic example of the deadly perils of managing train traffic with limited safety resources at the time.

George Barnes, conductor of train number two was bringing his passenger train up the west side of the pass. The train had been coupled in behind a three-engine freight, which had a rotary plow. They lost so much time in the snow that Barnes was worried because of a second freight train was following them by fifteen minutes. As they entered the Corona shed, Barnes prayed that his leading engines would pull them through to the east end of the shed before stopping or the second train might plow into the frail wooden passenger cars in the blinding smoke of the shed. Instead, the rotary crew signaled a stop at the first water and coaling station though provisions were made for water and coal further ahead. With the train prematurely stopped, Barnes sent his flagman into the gas-filled shed.

Ventilators (smoke exhausts) had been installed every few feet to carry the smoke out, but when a half-dozen engines were in the snow shed belching gas and smoke, the place was uninhabitable. Men passed out in the poisonous atmosphere and it became a dreaded place.

Section men were warned and even ordered not to walk through the sheds—even during storms—for fear that they would get caught in the blades of a rotary plow coming in the sheds. But who wants to walk out in a blinding blizzard? Men would gamble, take chances, and lose. Some would be caught by the large steam expansion cylinder of a locomotive as they crouched by the side of the icy wall. The remains would be picked up in pieces.

Barnes was uncomfortable recalling the numerous accidents and terrible deaths, and he must have spent time in reflection for those lost and their families and for the safety of his fellow workers.

The flagman was Jim Baker, a new man, whom Barnes immediately realized was unfamiliar with this snow shed. Realizing his mistake, Barnes dashed out with lantern and fuzee (a flare). As Barnes raced down the snow shed, the gas was so bad that his lantern went out. He passed the brakeman standing on the track without seeing him. Barnes could hear the second freight coming in from the west. He lit another fuzee and stopped under a ventilator. The air was better, and there he could see the snow bank on the sides above him on which he could stand, if he could get up there. He made a jump for the place and fell back. He spied a bridge spike on the wall of the shed. If he could somehow make a lunge for the spike and grab it, he would not be run over. He could hold on and brace himself in the snow and attempt to throw the fuzee in the cab of the freight engine as it passed.

Panting in the high altitude air and coughing from the gas, Barnes made a second desperate lunge, grabbed the bridge spike, and pulled himself up onto the ledge of snow, just as the engine came up on him. The smoke from the passing engine caused him to cough violently, and he could not throw the fuzee, but he did yell, as only a desperate man can. He heard the engine stop puffing. Earnest Anthony, the engineer, had closed the throttle. As the cab passed, he could hear the fireman holler "What's the matter?" Anthony replied, "I thought I heard a man yell."

Barnes was now opposite the first freight car. He climbed from the snow to the top of the car, crawled over the top to the front, and felt his way down the car's ladder. Coughing in the gas of Anthony's engine, he climbed up the ladder of the tender, crawled over the tank up the coal pile, and slid down the coal to the floor of the cab. He shouted, "For God's sake, don't move. I don't think you have run over my flagman." Coughing and gasping for breath, he told Earnest Anthony of the new flagman standing out there protecting his train. "Now don't move—no matter who tells you to move—until I come back."

The drama was not over yet. In the gloom of smoke and the thumping steam valves of the idling engines, Barnes had to locate his flagman who had trusted his life to his boss.

Barnes crawled out of the forward window of the cab and walked ahead on the runway to the front of the engine. What this gas must have been, we can only guess. Down on the track it had been heavy enough to put out his lantern. He climbed down the front of the engine and fumbled his way back. He literally bumped into his flagman, who was faithfully standing on the track, as Barnes had ordered. Jim Baker could not have been seen or heard by the engineer, and he would have had no escape.

Barnes and his charge walked back to the rear car of the Barnes passenger train, and the two sat down and rested. Baker was no doubt tired from standing and still may not have fully realized what had just taken place. Both were black with soot, carrying unlit lanterns.

Barnes, exhausted, was like a coiled snake, but he still possessed enough strength to proceed to the caboose in question, where he confronted the conductor and then moved on to the conductor of the snowplow, whom Barnes had trained, and tore into him. The crew had used shortcut operational procedures and poor judgment when they had pulled in for water and coal. The tie-up was finally untangled, but it took Barnes a long time to regain his composure. He resolved to never again place a passenger train between two freights. Had the second freight come into the snow shed and hit the passenger train, the wooden passenger coaches would have moved ahead into the first freight train where the brakes had been set, and the coaches would have collapsed on themselves. The passengers would have been killed in a raging inferno.[1]

# CHAPTER 12:
## RAILROADING

---

**A Friend Will Soon Be Gone**

Davi Moffat had a special railroad car fitted out for him that he would have coupled onto a train when he wanted to get out on the line to see for himself how things were going. At the end of the day, it was Moffat's habit to invite some of the crewmen to come to his car after they had closed down and washed up, and then they would dine together. The final visit may have taken place sometime around 1911 at Steamboat Springs, which was a favorite location for Moffat.

Bob Bishop, "Skeeter" Myers (his first name is not known), and George Barnes, reportedly two of Moffat's favorite engineers and conductor, had been invited to dinner. The evening would be their last time together. Moffat was to return to New York to again search for funding and investors. Edward Harriman had died in September 1909 at his home in Arden, New York, and there was no love lost between the two men. Moffat never forgot the offer Harriman made that would have given Harriman 51 percent of the control of Moffat's Denver Northwestern Pacific—and would have diverted the line north to connect with his Union Pacific line.

On March 20, 1911, Moffat collapsed and died in New York while trying to raise enough money to extend the line over to Craig,

Colorado. The tracks eventually did reach Craig in 1913, but never extended into Utah as planned. Years later, his line would join with other lines and reach Salt Lake City through Grand Junction, Colorado. A geological ally provided a shortcut through the north-central mountains of Colorado.

In hindsight, the cost of building and running the railroad over Rollins Pass was nearly as much as it took to build the six-mile tunnel ($18 million). Company records reveal that over $12.5 million had been spent just to get to Steamboat Springs, and the efforts had cost the lives of nineteen men. Perhaps the better strategy would have been to somehow find the financing and concentrate on the tunnel at the outset, but the placement of the tunnel had originally been situated much higher, which may have contributed to the hesitation of investors. The matter was really never resolved until the final location and effort to build the tunnel was determined. Later the Tunnel Bill legislation secured the completion of the project with a series of long-term bonds and the naming of the Moffat Tunnel Commission.

**Dangers in the Snow Sheds**

The smoke and gas fumes from the idling engines under gravity-drawn vents were seldom completely dissipated through the roof vents. Moreover, the drifting and falling snow would close up the roof vents until shoveled away. Men inside the sheds would suddenly collapse, and their coal oil lanterns would fail from lack of oxygen. Emergency treatment was pretty rudimentary, although it worked if the victim was carried out into the open air before too much time had passed. There should be no surprise that lung damage was pervasive, and many men suffered in their later years. Bollinger recalled a story on the lighter side about a fireman reportedly exposed to gas. Being overcome by gas in the snow sheds from the locomotives must have been a terrifying experience. All of the employees were at risk—as were the public passengers—if they lingered at the loading platforms while an engine was in proximity. The Moffat authorities, for good reason, had clearly defined safety rules regarding employee dependents visiting work areas. Nevertheless, a spouse of a station operator did gain access and subsequently witnessed the gassing of a locomotive fireman. The treatment procedure was simple enough. Lay the victim out on the floor with any available fresh air until he recovered. Apparently, the scene was more than the woman could tolerate and she returned from her quarters with a bottle of ammonia to hasten his recovery. The ammonia did its work when, with shaking hands, some of the liquid reached his nose. There was instant bedlam and property destruction as the fireman fought again for his life.[1]

Another employee reportedly confirmed the smelling salts story, and the terrible respiratory conditions in the snow sheds were well documented. Smoke masks had been experimented with, but were not particularly successful. It was not uncommon to find men unconscious or delirious in their engine cabs with rescue delivered at the last moment. Visibility in the snow sheds was poor or worse, and with blinding smoke and stinging gas, it was worse. At night, it was total darkness except the locomotive headlights. There is no historical mention or old photographs that show that electric lights were strung in the Corona snow shed, although electricity was available.

## Railroading

The railroad, for good safety reasons, established rules for crews to follow. Unfortunately, misunderstandings—and even neglect—would occur, sometimes with terrible consequences. Traffic coordination between trains moving over the pass was a challenge.

Electronic identification of train positions used by all lines today came into use after the tunnel was completed. Trains still operate under written orders prepared and delivered for a given trip—much like an aviation flight plan.

This is a coordination story reportedly from earlier interviews, which describes a long five-engine freight train from the west that pulled into the Corona shed to wait for a two-engine train coming up from the east, probably a passenger train. In the meantime, a second five-engine train from the west had pulled into the shed behind the first train and in the dark interior and hazy visibility from the smoke and gas, crept forward toward the unsuspecting caboose linked up behind the pusher engine and tender of the first train. A flagman had not been positioned behind the first train, perhaps because the fumes were so bad in the shed.

The second engineer, in the meantime, was looking for either a flagman or a fuzee as he slowly moved forward. Seeing neither, he continued ahead where he met up in the blackness with the caboose and coupled up. The annoyance of the stinging smoke and gas and poor visibility surely slowed down the reactions of the engine crew as the heavy engine, now coupled up, continued forward.

## Life on the Road

Non-crewmen were more or less on their own when they were sent out on an assignment. They missed the normal bonding between crews and they would grab rides on whatever unit was going their way. On this trip, a roadmaster was sleeping in the caboose of the first train, which was now being slowly crushed from the rear. Coupling two railroad cars is not a gentle action, and to crumple up a wooden caboose while it is held firmly in place by the brakes of a heavy engine must have been a terrifying experience for the sole occupant. The engineer in the pushing train said during a later accident inquiry that "he thought the rails were a little slippery, and when he felt resistance, he applied a little more throttle."

The roadmaster, now well awake, had enough presence to dash to the front of what was left of his space and attempt to climb the ladder up the back of the exposed engine tender. Too late. The snapping and shattering of the planks and timbers of the caboose caught up with him as the debris scattered in the confines of the snow shed. In some bizarre chance, a large nail embedded in one of the timbers caught in his trousers and the roadmaster was lifted up and over the engine tender.

At that instant, the nail must have torn loose, and he miraculously slid down the icy wall and rolled behind the tender and between the tracks. He trembled beneath the hissing monster that had just destroyed his resting place as it crept over him. He was certain that if he moved a muscle, the engine might scrape over him. The story ends with a hot coal reportedly falling on his chest, severely burning him and requiring hospitalization.

Men who work around danger often have a macabre sense of humor. After the roadmaster incident, non-crew members may have been reminded that they traveled at their own risk.

## Labor Management

Other roads observed the sixteen-hour law that mandated the longest period a railroad employee could work without a break, but Moffat executives deferred until much later. Ninety-hour work stretches were not uncommon. Frostbite and frozen extremities took their toll along with the infirmities that showed up in a man's later years. Most railroaders in those days did not enjoy a long retirement.

Working and living conditions on the line were often marginal at best. The Brotherhood of Locomotive Firemen and Engineers represented the crews for the most part. An August 26, 1919 grievance submitted through the Tabernash Junction shops offers some insight into crew conditions. The men wanted higher wages before anything, and to reinforce their requests, they submitted examples of safety, comfort, and faulty equipment. This was the period of wage restraints—and even reductions—as railroad management focused on doing something with the tunnel.

## Labor Pleadings

Dear Sir and Brother: "I am mailing under separate cover, the information that you have requested for the proposed increase in wages. I am also giving you an outline of the conditions that exist here." Author: There follows some lengthy remarks about locomotive maintenance and safety. "We have had a number of hard riding engines due to Quarterslip. They are more of the Mallet class. J. A. Higgins was pulled out of service for refusing to operate engine 307 to Tolland from Corona on August 5 and double back from Tolland to Tabernash, a distance 84 miles. This engine is one of the worst ones that we have had to contend with. On several occasions this engine had broken pipes and connections to the main reservoir. Losing all the air and when steam was used, the gasket on the valve chamber blew out. Engine equipped with a Raggonet gear leaving nothing at all to take this engine down a 4 percent grade." Author: the representative goes on to mention that the disciplined employee lost five days' pay and several other engineers lost time suffering from back and kidney pain. The complaint continued with snow sheds and fueling. Firemen will burn (shovel) sixteen to twenty tons of coal on a trip from Denver to Corona, a distance of sixty-five miles through thirty-two tunnels and six snow sheds. "The conditions of the sheds are bad and the one in Corona in particular. There have been a number of Brothers gassed and burnt in this shed and one of them died. As I was on the engine that fireman R. H. May died on, I can give you the exact facts of the case, which are as follows: Called at Tabernash at 2:00 p.m., left at 3:05 p.m., and arrived at Corona at 11:20 p.m. We followed a train into the shed. Both trains consisted of three engines each. The train that we were helping was stopped so that our engine was just at the end of the double track and the narrow part of the shed with ventilation.

"We stood there about 15 minutes when the gas and smoke became so thick that it extinguished the oil torch that I had burning on the oil tray, also putting out the lanterns. The Fireman said that it was sure getting thick and that he was getting weak. I gave him a cup of coffee that I had made before going into the shed."

Author: By now conditions were desperate. "He was then so weak that he could not take the cup from me. I held him so that he could drink it and he was getting weaker all the time. I picked him up and laid him with his head out the gangway, so that I could fan what fresh air I could get to him. I felt myself getting weak, so I laid him back against the coal gate and started to get to my side of the cab and whistle for help, and so place my-self that if I did go under, I would not fall against the fire box or doors. Instead of getting to my side of the cab, I fell out of the gangway, so that I lay with one of my legs under the tank hose and the other over the hose. This was the condition I found myself when coming to. When I got back in the cab the fireman was still breathing a little, but still out. I looked at my watch; it was 1:55 a.m., so you can see that I was out about two hours. The fireman from the rear helper had walked over the train. I called to him to get some help. While he was walking to the head of our train, another train started to pull up. It is impossible to see or walk except between the rails when there are any trains in the shed and there were three trains this night. This shed has always been considered not safe to make meets in [accommodate more than one train at one time]. The former management directed that only in extreme cases of emergency would any meets be made there, but even after this case had happened, present dispatchers continued to make meets at this point."

Author: Some safety procedures either were not followed or did not exist. "The helper engine firemen are required to turn their engines out at this point, which is very unsafe as the snow and ice will pile up so that a man has to stand on the rear tank sill as snow and ice will not clear him on the side. He has to ride on the sill to keep from being drug off the tank. They are not clothed to get down and dig out switches and ride around this shed after firing an engine up the hill, which means ten to sixteen hours without anything to eat, so you can see that it is very easy to be overcome while in this condition."

Author: Adequate rest facilities were another complaint. The writer complained that with the second district out of Tabernash "every train is a local and men cannot get anything to eat after 10:00 p.m. at any point between Phippsburg and Tabernash," and he continued with complaint that "the coal Chutes at Kremmling are not safe, nor elevated sufficiently and requiring the men to shovel 8–10 tons of coal into the tender rather than the coal simply rolling from the chute into the tender." Steam railroading is dirty work and there was griping about the lack of washing and laundry facilities.

"At Phippsburg there is one hotel and one rooming house run by private parties. The hotel is known as one of the dirtiest places in the country. Rooms are filthy, beds are never cleaned, there is no heat furnished to rooms whatever. Under the building there is a cesspool and the odor from it is very sickening. Conditions at this point are very poor and for the present time it does not look as though we would be able to have them improved. The meals at times when officials are here (which is seldom) are very good, but at other times the meals furnished are very poor. The rooming house is fair. If a person rooms at the hotel, meals are 50 cents, otherwise 75 cents.

Crews on the road at night have no place whatever to get warm meals, only a cold lunch carried by them."

Author: Apparently, the caboose and its minimal creature comforts were reserved for the non-engine crew members. Even the Denver buildings were reportedly lacking adequate crew comforts. An old unheated stone building at Utah Junction partitioned from some line offices was about the limit.

In Tabernash, a major division point on the line, complaints were again made about either lack of or satisfactory crew quarters. There were reportedly two hotels in Tabernash, and one was judged to be quite good and the other not so good. Griping and complaining by the crews was not necessarily a sign of serious discontent. It was a common theme among all railroaders then and now. The Moffat people though were a resolute group and perhaps "put together" a little better and tighter than their flatland cousins. The nature of their work and very existence pretty much demanded a more self-reliant individual.

Author: Pay schedules were implemented from time to time despite tight economic conditions, although not in the open and generous manner of David Moffat. For engineers and firemen, type of equipment operated and later seniority set the standard. An August 1912 manuscript disclosed a wage of $5.10 per day and $5.10 per mile. Firemen received $3.55 for each day and mile for the top class of equipment. The three classes were Simple Engineers, 137,000 pounds or less, probably yard engines; equipment over 137,000 pounds "resting on the driver"; and class three was the Mallet articulated compound engines used on the pass and elsewhere on the line. By 1919 the wage for class-three engineers had reached $6.34 per day and $6.34 per mile.

# Chapter 13:
## Moffat Legacy

M offat was impressed with the manner and style that Andrew Carnegie was endowing his wealth about the country, principally in the library system. He wanted to do something substantial for the Washingtonville and Blooming Grove communities that had served him well in his youth. The planning may have commenced with a meeting in Denver in 1885 with his cousin, John Newton. The details of the event are lost to history, except that Newton agreed to manage the project and did so until his death a year later. Hector Moffat took over and was followed by a succession of trustees and managers.

At first, various family properties were purchased and refurbished; some buildings were moved to form the basis of a compound, and the Moffat Library Association was formed with the formal dedication on June 1, 1887. Upon petition, the New York Legislature moved to establish an act that the library was to be a self-perpetuating corporation—an early-day tax-exempt organization. Over the years, the facility and its endowment have grown and served the general community and brought pride to the Moffat name in a host of ways.[1]

# CHAPTER 14:
# HONORABLE MENTION: GANDY DANCERS

The section men worked under difficult conditions regardless of the season. Gandy dancer is slang for a railroad worker in a section gang. The term originated from the tools he used, which came from the Gandy Manufacturing Company of Chicago.

When a rotary plow stalled at a twelve-foot drift or derailed, the section men had to lower the drift to ten feet with dynamite and shoveling, or re-rail the plow. Since the plow was so heavy, a crane mounted on a flat car after 1905 would be summoned. Extreme cold can cause steel to react strangely. Temperature swings can be great at high altitude—from an afternoon with a hot sun to an early evening when the mercury drops a degree a minute. In extreme circumstances, rails would sometimes snap. Section men managed a peculiar problem when, in the heat of the sun, the top or exposed part of the rail would break loose from the bottom part of the rail that was still buried in the ice. Since the trains usually moved at only ten to fifteen miles per hour on the pass, many potential accidents were avoided.

Rails come in different strengths, measured in pounds. The heavier rail refers to more weight-carrying capacity; the Moffat line, like most lines, gradually increased its standards. To lay a new rail, a replacement was pulled off a flat car and dragged behind the engine and then positioned and anchored into place. Day or night, weather—wet, snow, cold, windy, lightning—was a gandy dancer's companion.

Poor judgment on the part of a crew member, but especially the engineer or conductor, could tie up a line for hours or days. If an engineer thought he would be safe with the water he had and was trying to save time and passed up a refilling point, deeper snow than expected would erase his margin of error, and he could end up with a dead engine and a stalled train.

If an engine went dead for any length of time, an engineer and his crew had to drain it, which was a miserable job, and it was just as difficult to restart an engine.

Despite the normal griping, the Moffat employees, for the most part, gave the best of themselves. The Moffat line was eventually regarded as the best equipped and maintained and regularly passed its government inspections. Expenses were eating up the company and, by the early 1920s, the projected tunnel was becoming a more realistic alternative to the public authorities. More company funds were being directed toward the tunnel at the expense of railroad equipment and upkeep of the road.

In the meantime, 20 percent wage cuts were implemented in the late teens, and understandably, this hit everyone pretty hard. When Moffat was still alive, he was generally supportive of the men's demands. President William Freeman, who ordered the pay cuts, was not the gentle Moffat. Freeman drove the employees into a fury, and many left for easier times and better pay.

Poor pay or not, there was still a railroad to operate and Charlie Peterson, Denver yardmaster mechanic, went to work on a long-standing problem of ice buildup between the rails that would form a solid sheet and contribute to derailment. Peterson designed hydraulically operated "ice picks" that fit under a locomotive. They would gouge out the ice that formed after the rotary passed. A following rotary plow could then throw the ice up and out. The chisels were a hefty thirty inches long, six inches wide, and two inches thick. The hydraulic action would allow the implement to be raised while riding over switches and other sensitive obstructions.[1]

## Snow Slides

George Schryer, one of the first group of locomotive engineers, was posted at Tabernash (the first division point on the west side of Rollins Pass). He was regarded by his peers and managers as one of the best at his job. During the earliest era, Fraser was an assembly point for engines as well as Tabernash five miles west. But Tabernash soon had a repair depot because of more accessible terrain, and it became the main location. Sometime during the late 1940s, Schryer recounted to Bollinger a frightening incident that happened to him and his crew around 1912 or so while on a winter night run east over the pass. Moffat had died in 1911, and although he was still mourned, William Freeman was president and trying to control costs. He was pushing men and equipment to the limit.

Prior to the Schryer train's departure, there had been a huge tie-up on the line, and all trains were behind schedule. Finally, the five-engine and rotary plow coal train was approved to head east out of Tabernash for Denver with Schryer in the fourth engine. Bollinger recounts Schryer's compelling story:

Schryer had warned an official that a snow cone overhanging the track below the loop ought to be shot [dynamite then—now live small cannon ammunition is used to dislodge a potential avalanche]. "I guess the officials were afraid [President] Freeman would fire them for wasting time and powder." The coal train was composed of a rotary plow, three engines, and twenty cars of coal. George Schryer's locomotive was the third followed by the fourth engine and fifteen cars of coal, the caboose, and the fifth pusher engine.

Their orders were to wait at Ranch Creek for a passenger train out of Denver. It was to have pulled into the wye [a turn-around set of tracks]. But when the freight went through Arrow, it received new orders changing the meeting place to the loop [still on the west side of the pass].

At Ranch Creek, the five engines and the rotary plow each took on water. When all were ready, the plow operator whistled the usual two long blasts, followed by the other locomotives, which pierced the cold night air. The first engines with their drive wheels spinning lunged ahead at the hundreds of tons of dead weight, while the slack between the cars rumbled down the line. The rear engines met the moving slack and pushed against the descending momentum. Gradually, as the train was moving, each car found its place between the pulling and pushing engines. Author: Listening to a struggling engine—modern diesel or early day steam—getting a load moving is a sound all of its own.

Schryer had been selected to make this run, although he had just returned that morning from a trip a few hours earlier; he could have handed it off to someone. Instead, he agreed to the assignment, much to the displeasure and foreboding of his wife and their friend Susan Anderson.[2]

The latter was a remarkable medical doctor who only shortly before had been delivered to the Schryer home by train crew members to recuperate after being involved in a bizarre accident. She had fallen into an engine work pit at Tabernash and was lucky enough to have only painful injuries.

Dr. Anderson—known by the county residents as Doc Susie— lived at Fraser and was one of the two or three physicians in or around Fraser in the Fraser Valley. While Schryer headed out on his run, both women anxiously watched through a spyglass as the train worked its way up to the snow slide area and saw the engine headlight come on. Schryer had a hunch about the snow cone. When he was under it, he turned on his light, which reflected against the coal car ahead. His fireman asked, "What did you turn the headlight on for?" George replied that he "had a hunch the slide was going to let loose on them from the snow cone."

He said he "wanted to see it hit." Hardly five seconds followed before the slide did indeed hit the train. Schryer recalled crying, "Prepare yourself." Boulders and tons of snow slid down with tree trunks and still more snow and boulders ringing against the bell and steam domes with terrible thuds. The windows of the cab on Schryer's side were crushed as the snow piled in the gangway and windows, filling the cab. Coal cars could be heard rolling hundreds of feet down the steep mountainside. They sounded like dynamite explosions. Schryer and the others had no idea as to the extent of the slide beyond their immediate predicament, nor whether they would live or die. More of the slide struck; the engine started to turn over. It settled back on the rails again as more snow came in the cabin from the back curtain. Gas and smoke belched out of the fire door. The snow was over the stack. Schryer and his fireman tried desperately to stamp the snow down to keep above it. Schryer recalled the engine started to tip over again. A boulder struck the engine bell, making a sound like the toll of death, while another coal car broke loose, thundering down hundreds and hundreds of feet below. The engine settled back to the rails. The two men, still frantic, maneuvered about the cab to keep above the snow. Their heads were against the cab roof, the gas was terrible, and the engine was buried under the slide.

Often during disastrous moments, men will think of their homes and loved ones. Schryer, a Canadian, and his Irish fireman reportedly were no doubt shaken from their thoughts when a third onslaught of the slide struck with terrible force. It must have seemed an eternity before the engine settled back on the tracks for the third time. The heavy engine was buried under the snow, the gas and smoke choking them, but they were spared being hurled seven hundred feet to their death.[3] The two crew members were frightened, along with the other crews, but they set to work getting themselves out of their predicament. They dug for fresh air while an explosion of gas in the engine seeped into their confined area. The heat from the engine melted some of the snow around the smokestack, and the gas fumes were lessened as they crawled out into the open. They surveyed a sea of snow, debris, and the tops of a buried train. The second locomotive remained on the tracks, and its crew had climbed out, but the snow had piled up to the point that a misstep would carry a man over the side and down a steep incline to join the fifteen smashed coal cars seven hundred feet below. The slide had apparently missed the first, fourth, and fifth engines.

Another slide threatened, and both firemen uncharacteristically refused to work to help shovel out their engines, so the tasks fell to the two engineers whose engines had been struck by the slide. The work reportedly took fourteen hours, and with the help of other crew members, the freed train was backed down several miles to the rail yards at Tabernash. Schryer was not done though; he cleared the packed snow off his unit with an ax. It was piled six feet above his cab. Afterward, a wet and frozen man stumbled home to his relieved wife, who he had left the prior evening.

Doc Susie, still recuperating from her fall and broken ribs, helped Mrs. Schryer with her husband, who was now a patient. The passenger train coming up from Denver must have been saved by an act of Providence. Somewhere along the way, it was stalled; otherwise, the Moffat line would have counted its first passenger deaths.

The later report to President Bill Freeman in Denver revealed something about the driving character of the man. He inquired if any of the engines had been damaged or lost—but not a word about the well-being of the crews. Management knew well enough that the men who worked "on the hill" could not operate under distant rules; the twenty-six-mile mountain pass—and the overall operation—would simply fail in its tracks. So they were largely left to establish their own procedures within the company systems—and much to their credit, it was successful for over a quarter of a century.

## Dr. Susie Anderson

Susan Anderson, MD, arrived at Fraser for a two-week vacation in the summer of 1907 along with a train full of lumberjacks and a few tourists. She had graduated from the University of Michigan's medical school in 1897, and—like many people who came to Colorado—she suffered from tuberculosis. She had been working as a nurse in Denver (women doctors were still treated as second class). Recalling the peace and charm of the Fraser Valley, she returned on December 24, 1907. Her winter greeting was a little different from the dreamy alpine summer.

This time, Dr. Anderson hung out her shingle, and word was soon out that a new lady "doc" was in town. Her first patient was a horse brought in by his cowboy owner. The animal had gotten snagged and caught up in barbed wire and was badly lacerated. With the town quietly observing, she sewed up the numerous wounds and released him to his owner, promising she would look in on him. This brought about a hesitating respect that gradually grew into devotion.

On one occasion, she was summoned by an engine crew that stopped in front of her house—the usual practice. A crew member pounded on her door, calling her to see an engineer at Tabernash who was believed to be having a heart attack. She diagnosed the problem to be food poisoning after his fireman commented that the engineer had earlier eaten a "smelly and greasy sausage." Doctor Anderson believed sodium bicarbonate would relieve her patient. She was not the official Moffat company physician. However, the crews ignored that fact, and they carried her in the engine to wherever she needed to go, which might have been to a wagon or sled road siding where she would be picked up by a lumberjack and driven back into a lumber camp to treat the victim of an accident.

Once she accompanied a teenage boy to the Colorado General Hospital in Denver when she correctly suspected that he was about to suffer a burst appendix. In those days, there was not much in the way of antibiotics, and he would have died. The admitting staff began to hassle her and her country appearance, implying she and the lad did not belong there, but the chief of staff, who knew all about this country doctor at Fraser, immediately intervened, and the young man received his operation. The round trip was courtesy of the train crews. The Moffat authorities in Denver were probably never brought into the loop—or some preferred not to know. She did suffer a serious and potentially fatal accident on one occasion.

Her earlier food poisoning patient was "hospitalized" at the hotel in Tabernash. The building is now long gone, but at the time Tabernash was the location of the maintenance shops at the western side of the line. Still concerned about the heart attack comments, she flagged an engine and rode the five miles to Tabernash to see her patient. Afterward, anxious to get back to Fraser, she hiked in the dark along the tracks toward the lighted car barns in the distance, where she could ask a worker to hail a passing train so that she could ride home.

In the darkness, she somehow strayed too far into the work yard. The roadbed suddenly became open ties, which she fell through into the pit from which the engines were serviced. She banged her head on a steam pipe and also broke a couple of ribs, but that was not the worst of the problem. No one knew that she was there, and from time to time, an engine would be moved over the pit to dump its load of white hot ashes as it was shut down for maintenance or repair. She frantically stumbled along the sides of the pit until some startled workers rescued her.

Black with soot and aching in the ribs, she was taken to George and Mrs. Schryer's home to recuperate. They were close friends, and it was from there that the two women bid good-bye to engineer Schryer for his trip up the mountain to meet a snow slide that nearly cost him and his crew members their lives.

# CHAPTER 15:
# THE MOFFAT TUNNEL

<br>

C olorado Senate Bill No. 3 of 1922 was the legislative approval for the Moffat Tunnel District. The final cost would be over $18 million, largely paid for by a long-term bond issue. The six-mile (6.1) tunnel was "holed through" on February 18, 1927, and the first official train with dignitaries and company officers passed through on Sunday, February 26, 1928.[1]

Before enactment of the defining bill, the Moffat road nearly went under, and the likelihood of any tunnel being built was in doubt. After Moffat's death in 1911, a succession of fixes was tried. The Colorado legislature in the same year issued $4 million in bonds, but public resistance prevailed. In 1913, a local investor tried on two occasions to put together a public-private deal, but it failed to gather much interest. By then, the line was in receivership. A new plan, a voting pool of investors, was formed in 1917. The investors pledged to hold their investment for at least ten years, which met the approval of the secured creditors, but the plan fell through.

Later in 1919, a state railroad commission was formed to determine the best of three tunnel locations—one of which would be the existing location. Pueblo citizens studied the plan and, recognizing their weaker position, influenced its defeat. Pueblo, by its southern geography, was certain to lose its main line position, and several local railroad lines felt threatened when they thought they would operate under an Improvement District.

The Rollins Pass tracks were abandoned and finally pulled up in 1935. There is no available record providing information as to whether the road was ever used again prior to 1935 for excursions or emergencies, or even freighting before it was abandoned—it probably wasn't, although there is a story that a rotary snowplow reportedly would not fit in the tunnel. More likely, they did not want the risk of the thing in the tunnel and something going wrong, so they sent it over the pass, where it derailed.

During the final years of tunnel construction, management allegedly neglected the maintenance of the Rollins Pass roadbed, diverting funds instead to tunnel construction. Automobiles used to be able to drive the route, but it is now blocked at several upper points. One of these points is on the east at Needle's Eye Tunnel; another is on the west at a trestle. Hikers, of course, can walk the entire route. There are ongoing historical preservation efforts to restore automobile access.

**Extending West**

With the tunnel completed, the ongoing conflict between the Moffat line and the Rio Grande railroad—under the control of the Missouri Pacific—came to a head. The Union Pacific to the north of Colorado, knifing east and west across the western half of the continent, gradually lost interest in Denver and the mountain exploits that had yet to mean much beyond the state borders. Some may have regarded the Moffat line as a fool's mission.

The Rio Grande held some Moffat stock, but the Rio Grande was in receivership to the Reconstruction Finance Corporation, and the Moffat stock was being held by the government as collateral. Nevertheless, the Rio Grande leadership persisted in obstructing any Moffat advances using rights of way, construction, and easements— any legal means that could be raised. Dotsero was regarded by railroad authorities who were involved as the gateway to Salt Lake City and the Pacific. It would not be the Royal Gorge route out of Pueblo—or Moffat's route across northwestern Colorado. And the Rio Grande people were not about to permit a cutoff to be built. It may have been one of many points of antagonism with the Rio Grande to fight at every step of the way because—some forty years earlier—the railroad had lost out to the Santa Fe railroad in a race to build a line over Raton Pass at Trinidad on the Colorado border and on to Santa Fe, the Southwest, and California. The sting of defeat may have still been felt among the company, even though the Rio Grande went on into the agricultural San Luis Valley and the mining boom of the San Juan Mountains. The Rio Grande, after a costly fight, also prevailed over the Santa Fe with its claim to the Arkansas River route up through the Royal Gorge.

The Rio Grande struggled through its economic crisis, and in 1932, at the depth of the Depression, a Reconstruction Finance Corporation loan allowed them to move ahead and build the forty-one-mile Dotsero Cutoff, completing it on June 15, 1934. The Moffat people resigned themselves that it was the end of their transcontinental dreams. At Orestod, a connecting point on the Dotsero Cutoff, a switch had been built by the Rio Grande workers to accommodate their line to enter the tracks that had been laid earlier. June 13, 1934, became a pivotal day for the two parties. The Rio Grande "envoy" to H. A. Sumner, Moffat's chief engineer, remarked that the Rio Grande plan was to "exercise their contract to run their first train over the line."[2]

Reportedly, Sumner took the message quietly enough. Moffat officials had discreetly discovered that the Rio Grande owed Moffat $388,000. Sumner then came alive and roared that they would not be allowed to proceed until they paid up—by the end of the day! The money didn't materialize that fast of course, but by the following day, it was in Sumner's bank.

The dueling continued among the Rio Grande, the Burlington, and the Moffat lines over minute specifications as to which company crews would operate this and that piece of equipment, which specified tracks were to be used by whom, and a work schedule. It was actually a harbinger of future railroad problems. In the meantime, the Depression continued to take its toll, as did World War II later on. So did the debts that would not go away. Finally, the Moffat line passed to the Rio Grande in a merger on April 11, 1947. The Denver and Salt Lake was absorbed by the newly named Denver and Rio Grande. The old animosities gradually vanished.

## Some Shortened Histories

Sequence of the different railroad lines: Denver, Northwestern, and Pacific Railway Company. Incorporated July 18, 1902. Operational from June 23, 1904–April 30, 1913, when the line was sold at foreclosure to Denver and Salt Lake Railroad Company on May 1, 1913. Denver, Utah, and Pacific Railway Company, and the Denver and Salt Lake railroads merged in 1912 for one year. In 1947, the Rio Grande merged with the Denver and Salt Lake as the Denver Rio Grande Railroad.

Historical interviews were made by Bollinger in *Rails That Climb*, second edition, with some of the most respected employees: J. B. Culbertson, chief dispatcher, on July 10, 1948, and March 31, 1966; George Barnes, first conductor, February 10, 1948; LeClair Daly, train master, March 26, 1948; William Rush and Bob Bishop, engineers, March 29 and 30, 1948; Sterling Way, engineer, January 7, 1948; William Woods Sr., engineer, June 12, 1946.

In the 1960s, Forest Crossen—in *Western Yesterdays*—interviewed several of the employees, including George Crawford, air brake foreman, Luther Van Buskirk and Dan Crane, engineers, and early engineer, Bert Fullman, who started in 1911 as an engine watchman and then rose to fireman and engineer in 1917. Crossen interviewed Joe "J. B." Culbertson, chief dispatcher, who provided a wealth of insight as to what had taken place during the last twenty-five years. The Moffat line, by any standard of the time, was well equipped, especially when its relatively limited mileage was considered. The line owned forty-two locomotives by 1910 and fifty-nine by 1915, and it played a key transportation role during World War I. One engine was totally destroyed in 1923 at Ranch Creek on the west side; some of the scattered parts no doubt remain today.

The later Mallets were more efficient, and they were equipped with mechanical stokers, which was an immense relief from the physical work of constant shoveling as the train climbed to the top of the pass. Anatole Mallet was the French designer of the engine that carried his name. The small drive wheels driven by a unique boiler system delivered immense power when a 4 percent grade was considered the limit of traction for a steam engine. Robertson provides some schematic specifications of a 104-ton mallet engine.[3]

The Moffat line nearly went bankrupt again in 1921 while the tunnel was being built. The Tunnel Bill of April 28, 1922, authorizing a 6.1-mile tunnel, assured completion of the project.

## Train Accidents

A runaway train had to be a terrifying experience, and most accidents ended with injuries, loss of life, and damaged or destroyed property. The incident described here is one of only four that escaped disaster. It is from a *Rocky Mountain News* story during the winter of 1912 and was contained in Bollinger's book.

A twenty-two-car coal train headed east pulled into the Corona shed at one o'clock in the morning. After taking on water, it eased down toward Tolland and Denver. Soon after leaving Corona, the train started picking up speed, which was quickly noticed by the crew since ten or fifteen miles per hour was the general speed on the pass. At a subsequent accident review board, conductor Van Franklin recalled that about three or four miles below Corona, the engineer called for brakes with one short whistle. Van Franklin and his two brakemen, Oliver Akers and S. S. Cheney, manually set the brakes on the cars and crawled into the caboose. They estimated that the train was now moving fifty or sixty miles per hour.

Antelope Siding was a tiny spot on a half-mile or more level grade where they hoped beyond hope that the emergency brakes would stop the train. Below Antelope was a 4 percent grade, and the train would hurtle to its destruction, killing its occupants. The runaway was traveling fast, but hopefully not too fast for the three men to jump, and they agreed that they would cut their caboose loose and take their own chance, but none of the men could bring themselves to jump. As the train reached Antelope, it slowly screeched to a stop—the brakes had mercifully held.

The shaken brakemen and conductor must have viewed the world in a new perspective as they climbed down from their caboose. They discovered that the engineer and fireman had jumped earlier as the train was slowing. The fireman escaped with a broken collarbone. A subsequent accident report determined that the engineer was new and had panicked. The report said that he had overlooked applying the air brakes first but applied the emergency brakes before jumping to safety. Water freezing in the lines of the air brakes was a frequent problem, but that was not indicated in this report. On another occasion, one train ran nine miles before crashing and closing the line for several weeks. Several men were killed. Still, most employees soldiered on.

## Other Accidents

During Crossen's 1960s interviews, Dan Crane, a retired engineer, described how engine No. 100 had blown up in 1918 when the water level in the boiler had been too low for safe operations. He recalled an engine striking a large boulder and flipping over in the front yard of a section house and a startled family at Hot Sulphur Springs in 1917. Steam boilers, despite their wide usage, were still dangerous. Crane recalled one boiler exploding and leaving nothing but the lower frame and running gear of an engine.

Train orders to proceed were usually well written, but misunderstandings still occurred. George Crawford, retired air brake foreman, related the story of two crews either misunderstanding or operating under two different sets of orders. A freight engine and crew stationed at Phippsburg was sent to meet a switch engine at Oak Creek. The switch engine crew stationed at Oak Creek understood they were to meet the regular crew at Phippsburg. The recipe for disaster was in place. In a blind race to meet each other, the two crews finally met up during daylight hours. The switch engine ran into the one or two boxcars trailing behind the regular train, breaking up and buckling the wooden cars up and over the cab of the freight train that the switch engine had been sent to help.

Crawford recalled another time around 1924 or 1925 when a blizzard on Corona buried everything. One plow was stuck, and two plows were working on the other side. It was necessary to again borrow (lease) the Colorado Midland snowplow. Crawford remembered that it took six weeks for the crews to clear the tracks.

The weather was constantly cold, and there seemed no place to keep warm. It was too cold to change, and the men slept in their clothes while snow seeping in through small holes and cracks in the cars would pile up in mounds. Sometimes it was not a pleasant place to work.

Hundreds of accidents and injuries—and some employee deaths—occurred during the Moffat era. Fortunately, there were no passenger deaths or even severe injuries. A few notable accidents have been recorded by Bollinger, and there are many more in the archives of the Colorado Railroad Museum. Engine air brake lines had to be frequently purged or blown out to keep them from freezing in winter weather. In one instance, a train ran down for nine miles from Corona with frozen air brake lines before crashing and killing several crew members. Boulders breaking loose and rolling onto the tracks or into the train were a deadly threat (they still are), although modern detection methods exist today.

On April 23, 1942, engine No. 3600 was hit and derailed by a large boulder. The engine was demolished. On November 16, 1935, there was a sixteen-car-derailment at Rollinsville when the eastbound train went out of control after reaching sixty-five miles per hour. They say some of the worst accidents happen close to home. On September 27, 1938, a head-on collision occurred between two engines at Lowell Boulevard near the Utah Junction shop's facility.

The final years of operating over the pass were largely routine by Moffat standards. Procedures were in place based on the early trial-and-error incidents that the line experienced. Most, if not all, Moffat employees from the very beginning until it was over, with the completion of the tunnel, would agree that there was virtually no margin for error. And like most people who operate under dangerous conditions, they may have seemed to the casual observer to be confident, unassuming, and relaxed. They were mostly in their own way, but they were also focused on their work that was a cut above the rest.

# END NOTES

---

**Chapter 1**

1 Edward G. McLaughlin III, *The Library and Empire of David H. Moffat, Jr.* (New York: Historic Blooming Grove Association, 1987), 7–8, 19–23.

2 Manuscript collection, 1 October 1907, Moffat Library, Washingtonville, New York.

3 kathy@camps-computer.com, December 23, 2000

4 McLaughlin, 24–35.

5 Forest Crossen, *Western Yesterdays*, vol. 10 (Fort Collins, CO: Robinson Press, 1976), 1–4.

6 McLaughlin, 24–35.

**Chapter 2**

1 Glenn C. Quiett, *They Built the West* (New York: Appleton Century Company, 1934), 55–60.

2 Ibid., 168.

3 John B. Norwood, *Rio Grande Narrow Gauge* (River Front, IL: Heimberger House Publishing, 1983), 125.

**Chapter 3**

1 Glenn C. Quiett, *They Built the West* (New York: Appleton Century Company, 1934), 171–74.

**Chapter 4**

1 Dee Brown, *Hear That Whistle Blow* (Canada: Holt Rinehart, 1977), 57–59, 194, 190–93.

2 Dodge website: accessed March 23, 2004, http://www.linecamp. com/museum/americawest/western-names/dodge-grenville-mullen; http://www.users.quest.net/-dodge75/; http://www.rootsweb.com /-iapottaw/D.htm; http://www.depau.edu/library/archives/ijhof/ induct/colfax.htm.

3 Robert S. Riegel, *The Story of Western Railroads* (New York: McMillan, 1926), 145- 159, 141–43.

4 Gould website, accessed March 23, 2004, http://college.hmco.com/ history/readerscomp/.

5 George E. Kennan, *E. H. Harriman: A Biography* (New York: Houghton Mifflin, 1922), 1–3, 15–16, 61–65.

6 Harriman website, accessed January 19, 2006, http://www. thefreedictionary.com.

7 Michael P. Malone, *James J. Empire Builder of the Northwest*, (Norman, OK: University of Oklahoma Press, 1996), preface, 213– 25.

8 Minnesota Historical Society website, accessed February 7, 2011, http://www.mnhs.org/placer/sites/jjh/wikipediajames.html.

9 www.jpmorgan website/Wikipedia,accessed February,12,20,11http:// wickopedia.org/wicki/Jp_morgan.

10 Adams, Eugene H., Lyle W. Dorsett, and Robert S. Pulcipher, *The Pioneer Western Bank—The First of Denver*, 1860–1980, The First National Bank of Denver, N.A. and the First Interstate Bank of Denver, the State Historical Society of Colorado, Colorado Heritage Center1984).

11 Ibid., 26.

12 Ibid., 54–55.

13 Ibid., 51.

**Chapter 5**

1 Edward T. Bollinger, *Rails That Climb*, 2nd ed. (Santa Fe, NM: Rydal Press, 1950), 153–62.

2 Forest Crossen, *Western Yesterdays*, vol. 10 (Fort Collins, CO: Robinson Press, 1976), 4–6, 16, 19–20.

**Chapter 6**

1 Denver Municipal Facts. John Q. Rollins (Denver Public Library—Western History Section, v. 6–9), 19.

2 Forest Crossen, *Western Yesterdays*, vol. 10 (Fort Collins, CO: Robinson Press, 1976), 19–20, 5–6.

**Chapter 7**

1 Edward T. Bollinger, *Rails That Climb*, 2nd ed. (Santa Fe, NM: Rydal Press, 1950), 95–97.

2 Ibid., 99–101.

3 Ibid., 328.

4 Virginia Cornell, *Doc Susie* (Carpinteria, CA: Manifest Publications, 1991), 203–20.

3 P. R. Griswold, *Denver Northwestern and Pacific Railroad* (Denver: Rocky Mountain Railroad Club, 1996), 80–82, 100, 105, 164.

**Chapter 8**

1 Edward T. Bollinger, *Rails That Climb*, 2nd ed. (Santa Fe, NM: Rydal Press, 1950), 122–23.

**Chapter 9**

1 Edward G. McLaughlin III, *The Library and Empire of David H. Moffat, Jr.* (New York: Historic Blooming Grove Association, 1987), 107–08.

2 Edward T. Bollinger, *Rails That Climb*, 2nd ed. (Santa Fe, NM: Rydal Press, 1950), 233–43.

**Chapter 10**

1 Edward T. Bollinger, *Rails That Climb*, 2nd ed. (Santa Fe, NM: Rydal Press, 1950), 260.

**Chapter 11**

1 Edward T. Bollinger, *Rails That Climb*, 2nd ed. (Santa Fe, NM: Rydal Press, 1950), 272–75.

2 Forest Crossen, *Western Yesterdays*, vol. 10 (Fort Collins, CO: Robinson Press, 1976), 19–20.

## Chapter 12

1 Edward T. Bollinger, *Rails That Climb*, 2nd ed. (Santa Fe, NM: Rydal Press, 1950), 313–16.

## Chapter 13

1 Edward G. McLaughlin III, *The Library and Empire of David H. Moffat, Jr.* (New York: Historic Blooming Grove Association, 1987), 39–77.

## Chapter 14

1 Edward T. Bollinger, *Rails That Climb*, 2nd ed. (Santa Fe, NM: Rydal Press, 1950), 328–30.
2 P. R. Griswold, *Denver Northwestern and Pacific Railroad* (Denver: Rocky Mountain Railroad Club, 1996),72–74.
3 Bollinger, 301–02.
4 Virginia Cornell, *Doc Susie* (Carpinteria, CA: Manifest Publications, 1991), 47–49, 140–54.

## Chapter 15

1 Glenn C. Quiett, *They Built the West* (New York: Appleton Century 1965), 171-74.
2 Edward T. Bollinger, *Rails That Climb*, 2nd ed. (Santa Fe, NM: Rydal Press, 1950), 356, 329–31.
3 Donald B. Robertson, *Encyclopedia of Western Railroad History* (Dallas: Taylor Publishing, 1995), 118.

# BIBLIOGRAPHY

Ackerman, Kenneth D. *The Gold Ring.* New York: Carroll and Graf Publishers, 1988.

Bollinger, Edward T. *Rails That Climb.* 2nd ed. Santa Fe, NM: Rydal, 1950.

Bollinger, Edward T., and Alice Bollinger. "Big Snow on Rollins Pass," Colorado Magazine (Winter 1967).

Cornell, Virginia. *Doc Susie.* Carpinteria, CA: Manifest, 1991.

Crossen, Forest. *Western Yesterdays.* Vol. 10. Fort Collins, CO: Robinson Press, 1976.

Crossen, Forest, *The Switzerland Trail of America.* Fort Collins, CO: Robinson Press, 1962

Danielson, Clarence. *Basalt: Colorado Midland Town.* Basalt, CO: Pruett, 1971.

Davis, Elmer O. *The First Five Years of the Railroad Era in Colorado.* New York: Sage Books, 1948.

Denver Public Library, Denver Municipal Facts, Western History Section.

Griswold, P. R. *Denver Northwestern and Pacific Railroad.* Denver: Rocky Mountain Railroad Club, 1995.

Klein, Maury. *Union Pacific: The Birth of a Railroad.* Vol. 1. New York: Doubleday, 1989.

Kennan, George. *E. H. Harriman: A Biography.* New York: Houghton Mifflin, 1922.

McLaughlin III, Edward G. *The Library and Empire of David H. Moffat, Jr.* New York: Historic Blooming Grove Association, 1987.

Moffat Library. Manuscript Collection. Washingtonville, New York (October 1, 1907).

Moffat Society. *Moffatana*. Manuscript Collection of the Clan. Vol. 7, no. 3 (Fall 1992).

Norwood, John B. *Rio Grande Narrow Gauge*. River Front, IL: Heimberger Publishing House, 1983.

Pulcipher, Robert S., et al. *The Pioneer Western Bank—First of Denver*. Denver: First Intrawest Bank N.A./First National Bank of Denver, N.A., State Historical Society of Colorado, Colorado Heritage Center,1984.

Orange County Genealogical Society. *Early Orange County Wills*. Vols. 1-2. Goshen, New York, 1993.

Headley, Russell. *History of Orange County, New York*. Vol. 1. Goshen, New York, 1993.

Eager, Samuel W. *An Outline History of Orange County, New York*. Orange County Genealogical Society, 1847, 1995.

McLaughlin, Edward M. *Around the Watering Trough: A History of Washingtonville, New York*. Washington Centennial Cele. 1994.

Monroe, Gregory. *Moffat: Rio Grande-Southern Pacific-Union Pacific West of Denver*. Fox Publications, Arvada, Colorado, 1997.

Ormes, Robert. Railroads and Rockies. New York: Sage Books, 1963.

Overton, Robert. *Burlington Route*. New York: Knopf, 1965.

Quiett, Glenn C. *They Built the West*. New York: Appleton Century Company, 1934.

Ridpath, John. *History of the USA*. New York: Phillips-Hunt, 1881.

Riegel, Robert S. *The Story of Western Railroads*. New York: McMillan, 1926.

Robertson, Donald B. *Encyclopedia of Western Railroad History*. Dallas: Taylor, 1991.

Wilson, Spencer. *The Cumbres and Toltec Railroad*. Albuquerque, NM: University of New Mexico Press, 1980.

Yenne, Bill. *The History of the Burlington Northern Railroad*, New York: Bonanza, 1991.

## Electronic Bibliography

http://www.linecamp.com/museum/americanwest/western-names/dodge-grenville-mullen December 1, 2008

Kansas Heritage Group, Grenville Dodge, May 20, 20005

wickipedia james j hill, June 10, 2011

wickipedia E. H. Harriman, June 3, 2011

Minnesota Historical Society, http:www.mnhs.org/placer/sites/jjhh.aboutjames.html (2004)

Wickipedia jay gould, June 15, 2011

# INDEX